THE HOLY HOUSEHOLDER

LIVING A JOYFUL, ABUNDANT, AND SPIRITUALLY SATISFYING LIFE IN THE MIDST OF THE WORLD

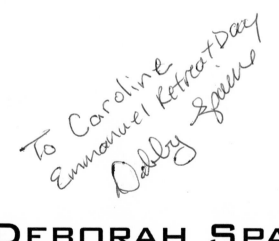

To Caroline
Emmanuel Retreat Day
Debby Spaine

DEBORAH SPAINE

outskirtspress

DENVER, COLORADO

The Holy Householder
Living a Joyful, Abundant, and Spiritually Satisfying Life in the Midst of the World
Copyright © 2013 Deborah Spaine
v2.0

Outskirts Press, Inc.
http://www.outskirtspress.com

ISBN: 978-1-4787-1523-8

Outskirts Press and the "OP" logo are trademarks belonging to Outskirts Press, Inc.

PRINTED IN THE UNITED STATES OF AMERICA

Acknowledgments

Many people have supported my writing of this book. My dear friend, Mark Rosenau, offered amazing quality assurance/editing recommendations to this project. Kathleen Townsend slugged through the first draft, offering supportive and helpful comments along the way. Pat Johnson read the final draft and assured me it was clear and told me it was "delightfully done." I thank these friends from the depths of my heart. Most important of all I thank my husband, Mal Schleh. He not only read numerous versions of this book, providing useful ideas and changes, but he offered his artistic and technical skills whenever I needed them. He was a comfort when I became discouraged, and a guide when I lost my way. Thank you. I also wish to thank Outskirts Press and the numerous people there who helped bring my dream into reality.

There are two points I would like to make for clarification. First, the examples of people I have used are fictional based composites of people I have known. Second, my use of the male gender when speaking of God is for literary and simplification purposes. God is intimately within us and hugely transcendent beyond our comprehension.

Table of Contents

Section I
The Holy Householder

1

Holiness

What is a Holy Householder? It represents something I have struggled with my whole adult life. How can I become holy, a saint, God's person completely, when living in the world, doing worldly things like being married, working, owning a home, sharing life with children, and so on? You know, a normal life. I was so inspired by all the holy people I read or heard about: St. Francis of Assisi, Mahatma Gandhi, Peace Pilgrim, Mother Teresa of Calcutta, Paramahansa Yogananda, St. Teresa of Avila, St. John of the Cross, Lao-tzu, St. Paul and so many more both modern and historical figures. They had clearly "made it," found how to move beyond their selfish selves, to be one with God, and to serve the Divine in this world. They are the predecessors on the Way. They give us a glimpse of what is possible and how best to get there ourselves. I yearned to be like them.

However, my impressions of how they lived their lives did not match up with how mine seemed to be evolving. I felt like I was not up to par on the spiritual journey. They all seemed to be focused on renouncing the world, being trained by strict disciplines of poverty, chastity, and prayer. St. Paul, the Christian apostle, says:

> *Now I say to those who aren't married and to widows—it's better to stay unmarried, just as I am. But if they can't control themselves, they should go ahead and marry. It's better to marry than to burn with lust.* (1 Corinthians 7:8-9, NLT)

Does St. Paul seriously believe the only reason to get married is to avoid burning with lust? Jesus teaches us to love one another. Much of his teaching is about having relationship with each other as the way to fulfill God's plan. Most religions put a lot of effort into guiding us in how to do relationship God's way—or the right way, according to their beliefs. Also, how would this world function if everyone were celibate and ascetic? I mean we need children in order to keep going as a species. What about joy? Jesus knew how to have fun. He provided for a great party. His very first miracle was at a wedding. He turned water into wine after everyone was already drunk on the cheap stuff. So what gives with this?

The uncertainty was very unnerving for me. It

required a lot of thought and struggle. I kept reading and searching. I did find some householder saints. The one that made me most hopeful was the father of Judaism, Abraham. He was so spiritually aligned with God that "the Lord" visited him in person, ate with him, and assured him that his wife, Sarah, would have a child that would take his seed into many future generations. Abraham was rich. He worked from home managing large numbers of cattle, sheep, workers, food supplies, and material goods. He was also asked to surrender to God's will in a way that most of us would find horrifying. He was asked to sacrifice his own child. Most amazingly of all, Abraham agreed to do it, and started the process of getting an altar ready and the knife sharpened. To everyone's relief God intervened and let him off the hook.

Abraham's story is a comfort to me because it demonstrates that our spiritual life is the life we are living right now. There is no spiritual life over here and daily life over there. They are one and the same thing. What I have come to understand is that the saints were called to their ascetic lives for a purpose. It was their path to become what they became. It is our path to become what we are called to be. Everything that happens in our daily life is grist for the mill of our spiritual life. It is the transformative yeast that lets us rise to the highest heights of who we already are: God's own beloved.

Everything we do to enhance our spiritual life aids the nurturing, molding force that makes us holy in the midst of the world. Our efforts to align our will to God's will, to live in line with the realities of truth and love, are deepened, challenged, and developed in the activities of our worldly life. We householders are already holy. Our holiness is inherent in our being alive. We have the Spirit within us. Are we, like Abraham, willing to live our lives with attention, care, and willingness to do what we know to be right even when it requires hard sacrifices? The more deeply and intimately connected with God we are, the clearer will be our purpose and potential in this world. We can develop that only from where we are.

∽∂∾

One of the first lessons in being a Holy Householder is the recognition that in this moment we cannot be anything other than what we are. That is the reality of life. If we can let go of all our judgments about what we should be doing, what we should have done, who we should be, how we should be, we would see that we are perfectly who we are right now. Everything in our lives has brought us to this moment, shaped and molded us. We are in process. As W.D. Wattles, the author of *The Science of Being Great* tells us, the world and each person in it is perfect, but not complete. We are perfectly who we are at every moment, but we are not complete. We are at our cutting edge of growth and development. The amount of energy, thought, time, and love we put into developing ourselves is what determines how slowly or progressively we grow. We are going to grow regardless.

We are also going to die regardless. We have limited time on the earth. It is for us to decide what we are going to do with it. What we decide can be accomplished only in the moment where we are right now. I cannot accomplish being holy by fantasizing about other people's lives and thinking I have to live just like them. The saints invested in their lives and they found their way. Their struggles were related to what they needed to learn. Our struggles are exactly what we need in order to learn. As householders, our struggles and challenges appear somewhat different from the saints', but in truth they are still the same lessons. Love, joy, peace, patience, gentleness, goodness, kindness, faithfulness, and self-control (Galatians 5:22-23) are the same fruits and requirements of the Spirit, no matter what kind of life we are living. Remember, this life is a precious, time-limited gift. We need to live it from where we are, and participate in where we are headed.

∽◌∾

It is up to us whether we will choose to live out our holiness as householders consciously or unconsciously.

If we choose to live consciously, our lives will be the greatest, most exciting, most fulfilling adventure we can imagine. If we choose to live unconsciously, we will still get dragged along toward our holy natures, but it will be much slower and a lot more painful.

Have you ever gotten a shot in the butt? If we tighten up and resist the needle, it really hurts those fighting muscles. If we relax and accept, it slips in and out with hardly a tweak. We get all the good stuff with much less pain. Becoming consciously aware of our own holiness by accepting and relaxing into it does not mean we become passive. Acceptance sees reality clearly. It comes fully informed and prepared for what to do next.

We live with the choice of what we will do next. We cannot change the past. We cannot control the future. Here lies our power, strength, and courage: we can choose what we will do next. The one thing we seem to most fear is the responsibility of living our lives fully. We fear taking up our power and choosing to live our lives as the Spirit guides us in truth and love.

This book is about how to relax, accept, and participate in our own holiness as householders. It is about facing our fear, taking back our power, and fulfilling our purpose in this life. There will still be pain, because it is hard for us to let go, surrender, discipline ourselves, and deal with the challenges and grief inherent in a normal life. However, the pain will be softened by the joy and deep spiritual support that are always there for each one of us. We are not alone. God is with us. Be not afraid. In fact, get excited, because what you are about to read will help you live a more fulfilling and joyful life. You are about to learn how to live as a Holy Householder.

2

Prison

It took me a long time to accept that I did not have to be an ascetic in order to be holy. Intellectually I could acknowledge it, but in my deepest fantasies I still believed the only way to be one with God was to go off to the desert, the mountain, the road, living simply, unattached, focused solely on prayer. I still believed I had to face demons the way St. Anthony did: living in a desert fortress for twenty years in complete solitude, getting beaten up by demons, and coming out holy. I still held the fantasy that I would need to go barefoot and poor like St. Francis of Assisi, a Christian saint after whom a religious order was founded. Minimal material goods and no worldly attachments still seemed like the only real way to God, which is the way the modern day holy person, Peace Pilgrim, did it. She walked back and forth across the United States then into Mexico and Canada, proclaiming the way to peace, owning nothing but a comb, toothbrush, and letter-writing materials, which she carried in her pockets. At best I would have to be like Mahatma Gandhi, married but celibate, saving a whole country from repression by living a radically simple life and speaking up to lead his people.

In my fantasies, these people never stopped at Starbucks to get a latte, or Nordstrom, or even JC Penney for just the right pair of pants. They never slept in on a Saturday to cuddle with their honey. They never indulged their desires. I did read once that Peace Pilgrim ate an ice cream cone, which was comforting, but still in my heart of hearts I felt that the celibate, ascetic life was the only real way.

This was a problem, because I got married at age nineteen. I married a man who was on his way to seminary to be an Episcopal priest. My mother was dying of cancer at the time. My father was an alcoholic, and once my mother was gone he was unlikely to put much effort into a relationship with my siblings and me. I had left home, an Air Force base in Georgia, to go to college in Oklahoma. I was lost and more than a little frightened, though I was not admitting this to myself.

There were two precious gifts my mother gave me. She raised me with the certainty that God is real, and the certainty that I am loveable. I was driven by the desire to develop both. I wanted a deeper, fuller relationship with God, and I wanted to be loved. Who better than a priest in training?

After eight and a half years of marriage, I went through a painful though mutually agreed-upon divorce. With my new freedom I went to graduate school for a PhD in clinical psychology. At the end of graduate school I met a man who was, as God told me quite clearly, the man for me. After a lot of therapy I agreed with God's point of view. I married again, choosing a householder's life once more. All of these choices shaped and molded me into who I am today. I know that where I am right now is perfect, though not complete.

I do not regret anything that has happened in my life. I learned early to listen for God's guidance. I know that He (Use of the male gender for God is for literary purposes and simplicity.) transformed even the limited and ignorant choices I made into something good. I have grown tremendously through all the stresses and strains of life. I believe that each experience had its purpose in teaching me how to choose more wisely.

So what finally convinced me that I do not have to be living a monastic life to be holy? Going to prison did it.

◦◦◦

After twelve years in full-time private practice as a psychologist, I began to yearn for a change. A Chinese fortune cookie told me, "Be not afraid of growing slowly, be afraid only of standing still." I felt like I was standing still. Other fortune cookies (I was eating at

Panda Express a lot in those days) were inspiring but also frustrating, "Use your natural talents to obtain more." "There is a prospect of a thrilling time ahead for you." Though I was chomping at the bit, wanting to move forward, God kept telling me to wait and be patient. I accepted this, but it did not change the increasing frequency of a rising energy inside of me that ached to move on.

During that time I was reading a lot of books about finding my purpose, becoming successful, and focusing my thoughts on the details of what I wanted in order to live my dream life. I had experienced a lot of bizarre coincidences in life that could be interpreted only as God's interventions, so it was easy for me to believe what I was reading. I started writing down and imagining work that was close to home (I had been commuting an hour each way for my private practice), that made at least $100,000 a year, that allowed me to work with a team of people doing a variety of activities like leading groups, teaching, and working with individuals in therapy. I also imagined this as a spiritually based work.

Out of the blue and to my surprise, I suddenly had the thought of working at the prison that is in the same town in which my husband and I had built our dream home. I had lived there twelve years without ever considering working at the prison. I had previously worked at a state mental hospital and actually liked the work. Strangely, the prison had a lot of what I was asking for in my dream imaginings. It paid as much as I had imagined, plus benefits. It was only about fifteen minutes from my home. I assumed it would be a lot like working at the hospital (my ignorance).

When I mentioned the possibility to other people, including my husband, they all pretty much freaked out and warned against it. Their reactions were so strong that I tried to let it go, but every time I tried to back off I would get this inner siren singing joyful music with lots of light and color, as though I were contemplating Disneyland rather than working in a prison. Needless to say, I was praying my heart out about this one. I just could not shake the inner certainty that this was where God wanted me to be.

∽◈∾

When I finally followed the call and was hired, I had the clear premonition that I was imitating St. Anthony. Like him, I was going out to meet the devil in his stronghold and fortress, the place where he and his demons hold sway. I felt my mission was going to be to bring light to a dark place. I had a vague idea that there were likely to be spiritual attacks on me, but I also felt certain that I was going in as God's own and He would protect me. I was guessing, but I felt pretty certain that this was going to be my opportunity for purification and service. Boy, was I right. Thank God we never really know what we are getting into ahead of time, or we might never be able to go forward.

For those of you who do not know St. Anthony's story, I encourage you to read Fr. Thomas Keating's version in *Invitation to Love*. St. Anthony was a fourth-century Christian who helped establish monasticism. Anthony started out a well-to-do householder but lost his parents when he was about eighteen. Inspired by a sermon, he sold all he had and began living an ascetic life. First he lived with very few material comforts and struggled with demons much in the way Jesus did in his forty days in the desert when tempted by Satan (Matthew 4:1-17).

After holding out against this initial assault, he decided to up the ante by going to the tombs, which in his day were considered the stronghold of the demons. He took his spiritual battle into the devil's territory. He got pretty badly beaten up out there, but held firm. After twenty years he came out filled with God's Spirit.

A significant difference between St. Anthony and me is that he went into the devil's stronghold isolated and alone. I, on the other hand, had my householder life to support and sustain me. My husband, after his own spiritual battle over it, also came to work for the prison. Together we pulled out our spiritual tool kits—or perhaps they could be called our armament. Each morning, after our morning meditation together, we prayed Ephesians 6 from the Bible about putting on the armor of God. As I walked onto the yards where

I was working, I would pray Psalm 23. During that time I learned that the fruits of the spirit mentioned above are not only the result of a spiritual life, but also the requirements of one. At the end of each day, my husband and I would sit in our beautiful meditation garden processing our days and meditating our way back to balance.

Just a warning: God gives us what we need in order to grow, especially when we have committed ourselves to doing so. In many ways, I had gotten what my thoughts had conjured up for a dream life. It really was a spiritual experience, with people to work with, and a variety of activities, but it was not what I had meant by that. Spiritual attacks came quickly and consistently throughout my time there. By the third year, they had increased to the point of being a noticeable pattern. There would be a period of ugliness, where usually nice people would suddenly turn aggressive and hostile. Officers would act out their frustrations more than normal and refuse to open the electronic doors to let me in or out. My caseload would go to an excessively high level, making keeping up with the work, let alone any quality, almost impossible. Officers would be abusive to inmates. Inmates would be abusive to officers. The people higher in seniority would make ineffectual decisions about what had to be done. The overwhelm of it all would get to me and I would think, "I have to get out of here!" When I was the closest to calling it quits, the whole thing would back off for a few days to a few weeks. I would start thinking, "I can do this. I could even like this." Then another bout would begin.

I started to believe that the devil did not want me to leave. He was having too much fun abusing me, God's person, in the midst of his stronghold. Naturally I continued to look to God, and here is what happened. I was able to keep my own center and act in the ways I valued. I used the fruits of the spirit as my guideline and acted with love, joy, peace, patience, kindness, goodness, gentleness, faithfulness, and self-control. I had not known I was capable of that for such an extended period of time. I could also see that I was indeed a light in a dark place. I saw both staff and inmates respond positively, more calmly and lovingly themselves after being around me. I de-escalated many situations that could have gotten really ugly and out of hand. I helped a few people choose the light over their darkest thoughts.

✺

For the most part, inmates are broken souls. They are crippled by heavy drug use since childhood, early exposure to severe and sustained violence, and head traumas from gunshot wounds, beatings, and accidents related to high-risk behaviors. Many of them have symptoms of Attention Deficit Hyperactivity Disorder: poor impulse control, poor attention, and excessive energy. Their insight is poor and their judgment poorer. They are trying to survive twenty-four hours a day in a place that was sapping me dry after ten hours a day, four days a week. Most of them have spent so much of their lives enmeshed with the darkness that they no longer know what is normal. Many want to believe in the light, but no longer trust it. Channeling the light by being present to them, showing care and consistency in my behavior, and always treating them with respect, I offered them a glimpse of another life where light can be lived with joy and peace. I even got to help some of them grow.

I was not alone in trying to be a light in the dark place. There were many other truly good people there, but the place kept us so busy or so spread out that we never united as a force of spiritual strength. Consequently, I began to burn out. What had started as a glow from my heart outward turned into a candle flame flickering unsteadily. At first I felt guilty about this, thinking I was blowing it somehow. My householder friends encouraged me and pointed out it really was an impossible situation. There was one time when I was begging God to let me leave the prison. I got the distinct impression that God gave me permission, but He also made it clear it was not His timing. So I stayed until God gave His permission freely and with certainty in my heart.

Since leaving, I have been able to more fully note the great gifts God provided. One such gift was that my husband and I paid off all our debt, including our house. As a householder, this is a satisfying accomplishment. He provided this right at a time when the economy came crashing down and many people were losing their jobs and their homes and living on unemployment. It allowed us to take time off on sabbatical to rest, heal, and pursue creative projects.

St. Anthony came out of the devil's stronghold a holy man. I came out a more spiritually enriched human being. I also finally understood and accepted that where I am in my personal development is just where I need to be. God has full awareness of the curriculum that is best for me to become complete, which to me means being completely His. As far as those holy people who have both inspired and taunted me, I realized they too struggled and doubted their own sainthood. Gandhi felt like a failure when India and Pakistan separated. Teresa of Calcutta's journals show that she had many spiritual doubts. Francis of Assisi separated from his own order because of conflicts. St. Teresa of Avila reportedly said to God, "If this is how you treat your friends, no wonder you have so few."

Being a householder is a calling. It is as valid a path as any other spiritual path. What is important is our participation in our evolving lives. Are we giving ourselves the best opportunity to be whole, to be complete, to grow into Holy Householders? Or are we just drifting along, living what life brings without trying to give God the chance to transform the lead of our lives into gold? Mother Teresa of Calcutta urged us to live an ordinary life in an extraordinary way. Are we willing to strive for this?

There are tools to help us in our endeavor to grow in our holiness. Ultimately it is grace that makes the changes in us, but there are ways for us to explore, understand, and participate in the process. This book is about the ways in which we participate in our spiritual growth. These same skills allowed me to deepen my experiences in life, including my experience in the prison, and to take leaps on my spiritual journey. I want to offer you the chance to leap as well.

Section II
Prayer

3

Values

What we value is that for which we are willing to make sacrifices. Remember, Abraham loved God so completely that he was willing to sacrifice his son. When we know what we value, we can begin to live our lives consciously. When we live our lives consciously, we find there is time and energy for everything we need. It all ties together. Knowing what we value allows us to prioritize our time and energy in such a way that we willingly let go of anything that does not fully give back to what we value.

As householders, our lives are filled with the demands of a life lived in the world. We often feel overwhelmed by the responsibilities to which we are committed. What comes first: our child getting off to school, our spouses' request that we do a task at home, our job asking us to come in early to finish a project, our church, friends, and family members wanting us to spend time with them?

We have to realize we have only so much time in a day. We have only so much energy to offer. We have only so much life left to live. The need to prioritize what we truly value is one of the most overlooked requirements in a householder's life. Not only do we avoid prioritizing, we avoid figuring out what we value. We just keep barreling along, doing what is put in front of us, doing what we believe needs doing.

I made a commitment, a very conscious choice that in my life relationship will come before doing. When I am washing the dishes and my husband comes up behind me to hug me, I turn off the water, hang my soapy hands over the sink, and lean back into his hug, soaking up the love that he is offering. In my early years I would have gotten irritated that he was interrupting my doing the task before me. I know better now.

⤙৹ঌ⤚

It is fun to determine what we value. It means asking, "What do I really want? What do I truly care about? What feels right to me? What makes me happy? What are the things in my life that make me feel like singing and dancing with joy? What makes me feel good about being me? What are the things that make me feel right with the world?" When we figure these things out, a natural burst of energy and motivation comes with them. They are a delight and joy. They feel like play. Even when they are hard to do, the rightness of them gives us inner peace and pleasure.

Once we have determined what it is we value (an ongoing process throughout our lives that often changes in depth and meaning as we grow), then comes the hard part. We have to choose what to do with all those other demands that do not align with what we value. If we have never tried to clean up or prioritize our lives before, we are likely to find that a huge hunk of our time and energy is going to people and activities that do not align with our true values.

Remember at the end of Chapter 1 when I told you this book is about facing our fear, taking back our power, and fulfilling our purpose in this life? I told you then that there would still be pain, because it is hard for us to let go, surrender, discipline ourselves, and deal with the challenges and grief inherent in a normal life. Here it is. Cleaning up our lives in order to live what we value takes a lot of courage and strength.

Sharon worked as a secretarial assistant for the owner of a small company. It was such a small operation that she, the owner, his wife, and a technician were the only employees. She had been with the company since it got started in the town where she lived. She had always loved the job. She felt like the people working there were her second family.

Then her boss started becoming more demanding.

At times he was sexually inappropriate, but in such subtle ways that it was hard for her to be sure. He would leave his hand too long on her shoulder, or stand a little too close when she was sitting at her desk. At other times he would keep her after hours for work, but then wanted to talk about how badly his marriage was going.

She also began to notice some of his business practices were not quite honest. He had a big money partner, and they would say things about their business dealings in front of her as though she were not there. She became very uncomfortable.

Little by little, the work environment became more and more intolerable for her, yet she was very committed. She also needed the money, and in her town there were not that many well-paying jobs. She became so stressed and overwhelmed that she came to therapy.

Sharon had to look very hard and honestly at what she valued and the ways in which the job was violating those values. It was a painful process for her, but eventually she and her husband decided to follow a dream they had, which included moving to the coast where they could live by the ocean and start their own business.

What is really good about cleaning up our lives is that acting on our own behalf builds strength and courage along the way. We do not have to start out as courageous giants. It is all a process. We have to have only enough courage to start. Sharon chose to come to therapy as her first step. In the story *The Wizard of Oz,* the Cowardly Lion had the courage to go on the journey with Dorothy in the first place. That was all he needed to start. He then discovered he did in fact have courage when what he valued was threatened. Just take the first step and keep walking. Our courage and strength will develop, as we need it.

4

Praying

The first step in spiritual life is prayer. Prayer is the opening of the heart and mind to God. Imagine you are in the middle of working on a project that is totally absorbing your attention. Suddenly your four-year-old daughter comes over to you, wanting to say something. At first your mind and heart are closed; you are irritated about being disturbed. However, you are a good parent, so you stop what you are doing, give your child your full attention, and ask what she wants. She looks you right in the eye and says, "I love you." Suddenly everything that was tight and resistant melts inside of you, and your heart and mind open fully to this tiny person who is offering you a precious gift. You have been opened by love. Prayer is like that.

Conscious prayer is a discipline, a choice we have to make to pull our attention away from our projects and give it to what we value. It can feel like a burden when we are already overwhelmed by too many relationships and too many requirements in our worldly lives. Why would we want to add more to our busy schedules? When we receive the gift of love, as in the example above, the effort is nothing compared to what we get for having done it. Such an experience brings awe, a sense of intimacy, and a softening within our souls. We feel loved.

It goes back to what we value. Peace Pilgrim tells us:

If your life is in harmony with your part in the Life Pattern, and if you are obedient to the laws, which govern this universe, then life is full and life is good but life is never more overcrowded. If it is overcrowded, then you are doing more than is right for you to do—more than is your job to do in the total scheme of things.

Getting into harmony with our lives can be done only through prayer, the opening of our hearts and minds to the Spirit who guides us. Listening for God in our hearts is essential to finding the balance in our lives that will allow us to live our values. It is like the story above where the child comes to us saying, "I love you." If we do not take the time to hear our own inner voice saying that we are loved, or we refuse to pay attention to the message of our hearts, we will live with a constant strain of resistance—like resisting the shot in our butts that I mentioned before. We may also miss the opportunities that lead to our true purpose because we are too blind or busy to notice them.

On the other hand, if we do commit to prayer, we will find ourselves drawn toward a more meaningful and fulfilling life. God is eager to have us align with His will. Peace Pilgrim calls this alignment being in harmony with the Life Pattern and the laws of the universe. Other religions call it being fully awake or enlightened. It means taking back responsibility for our lives. It means making a choice to pursue that which will give us the best results for our time and energy.

❧

Let us say you decide to go shopping (or as my husband and I joke, for a man it is research). When we make a plan for our time and energy, are we willing to ask, "Why am I doing this?" If we truly need something that we must go buy, then by all means take care of business. However, for many of us the activities we do are fillers, a way to "kill time," or a way to feel like we are giving ourselves something special. It is disturbing to me that research indicates Americans watch more than four hours of TV a day. Why do we feel the need to escape from the lives we are living? Peace Pilgrim suggests that when we live in harmony with what is true and real, we no longer feel the need to get away on a vacation. What she is suggesting is that when we are in harmony, our lives are more peaceful, full, and joyous. We no longer need to escape from them. What about the people with whom we spend time? Are there people in our lives that we hope will not call us, or whom we avoid when we catch a glimpse of them in public? Are we doing activities that we dread having to go do? Have we asked ourselves why are we doing them? Some people and some activities are a sacrifice for love, and therefore represent something we value, such as taking our kids to Little League and hanging out with the other parents to watch the game. I would bet, however, that there are many people and activities that we do not want in our lives, but we do them anyway because we are afraid of hurting someone's feelings, or looking bad, or we have trouble saying "no." (We will discuss this more fully in Section III on relationships.)

What relationships are most important to you? Is God on that list? Is your spiritual life on that list? We have to choose. Do not choose out of guilt, "should," or "have to." We must learn to choose out of what our hearts are telling us. Our hearts are a sure connection to God. When our hearts sing with the rightness of something, we can be pretty sure it is of God. When our hearts shrivel up and pull away from something, we can be pretty sure it is the wrong thing for us. Of course, sometimes we force ourselves to do something our hearts pull away from because there is a greater good, like going to treatment for cancer, or my husband going to work at the prison. When we stop to listen for guidance and direction, we will know the difference.

∽◇∾

Prayer is about relationship. It is about interacting with Spirit in whatever way we may experience that universal power of love. Relationship requires our time and attention. The more time and attention we give to anything, the more intimately connected we will be to it. The more connected we are, the deeper and more responsive will be the relationship.

Because I am Christian, a personal relationship with Christ has been my path to the Spirit. I was eleven years old when I first fully acknowledged my commitment to my spiritual path and to Christ as my Way. I consciously opened my heart and mind to God. In a very short time I experienced a number of unusual experiences that confirmed for me that the path to which I had committed was true. At age twelve, I was sitting in a Sunday school classroom waiting for the other students and the teacher to arrive when I felt a powerful presence in the room. It seemed like it was located in the top right corner of the room near the ceiling. I had no words for this. I knew only that a loving, benign presence was in that room with me. I cried with the awe of it. I felt honored and loved.

My Angel in Astoria

Another time I was on my bicycle in a neighborhood I did not know. I was lost, my bicycle chain had broken, and some older boys rode their bikes by me, taunting me and calling me names. I had no idea what to do. So I stopped in the middle of the street, bowed my head down on the handlebars, and prayed. I asked God to help me find my way home. I kept walking. The next cross street was one I knew would lead me home.

When I was eighteen years old, I had come home from college for the summer. Near our home in Georgia was a golf course with manicured lawns and well-trimmed trees. Late one night I was restless and unable to sleep. I went into the night, passing through the deep shadows of magnolia and pine trees that lined the streets. As I entered the golf course from the road, I was hit with an experience so intense and overwhelming that no words could do it justice.

Afterward, I put words to it the best I could. I saw a tall pine tree standing alone in the white light of the moon. Suddenly, I knew, experienced, that the tree and I were one. The moonlight and the shadows were all me and I was the moonlight and the shadows. There was no separation or difference between anything I could see and me. We were all one. Then another wave of realization hit and I knew with absolute certainty that all that oneness was God. God is everything and everything is God.

We cannot predict or make these experiences

happen. We cannot force relationship with God on our own terms. God comes to us as pure gift. I had been raised to say grace before dinner, a child's prayer before sleep, and to attend church—saying the church prayers, usually from a book. I had tried in college to meditate using bits and pieces of instruction, like staring at a candle or repeating a Hindu phrase. None of these are what gave me an experience of God. What made it possible was my hunger to deepen my relationship with God. What made it possible was my opening my heart and mind to God even when I had no clear idea of how to do this.

5

The Breath Prayer

The simple yearning in our hearts for greater intimacy with God is our first prayer. God always answers this prayer. There is nothing more pleasing to God than our desire for Him. In order to deepen that intimacy, we need to find ways to reach out more consciously. We need to make ourselves available to the Spirit.

Over thirty years ago I learned a form of Christian meditation called the Breath Prayer. The use of the word breath is based on the idea that our prayer is as vital to our spiritual life as our breath is to our physical life. It brings together the three definitions of the Hebrew word *ruach*, which can be translated as breath, spirit, or wind. God's breath blown into us is what enlivens our spirit. This form of prayer was developed and taught by an Episcopal priest named Ron DelBene.

Prior to learning this form of Christian meditation,

my effort at conscious prayer had been a matter of talking with God or saying formal prayers, reading spiritual material, and sitting quietly listening, though I found it difficult to stay focused. In college I had tried using the Hindu mantra *OM*, but never felt comfortable with it. I had been giving daily time of quiet to God, but my attention was scattered and vague. The Breath Prayer gave me a focused, specific way to participate in a deeper relationship with my inner heart. It gave me a way to tame my wildly busy mind so I could more intimately listen for God's voice within.

I especially like this prayer because it was developed out of my own spiritual tradition. It was not borrowed from other religions. A whole tradition of Christian spiritual practices developed after Jesus walked the earth, all aimed at deepening our experience of God through Christ. There is a lot of overlap between the deeper, more mystical practices of most religions. However, each religion bases the intent of the practices on their particular belief system. Christian prayer practices focus on opening the mind and heart to Christ.

The Breath Prayer is a repetitive prayer that uses a phrase that is personal to the practitioner. The chosen word or phrase is said silently over and over. In some Eastern traditions this is called a mantra. It is *not* a mindless repetition to make our minds blank. Rather, it is a way to focus our thoughts on the intention to be present and receptive to God. God is always with us. The prayer helps us to open to that reality.

I can never escape from your spirit!
I can never get away from your presence!
If I go up to heaven, you are there;
If I go down to the place of the dead, you are there.
If I ride the wings of the morning,
If I dwell by the farthest oceans,
Even there your hand will guide me,
And your strength will support me.
I could ask the darkness to hide me
And the light around me to become night
But even in darkness I cannot hide from you.
To you the night shines as bright as day.
Darkness and light are both alike to you.
(Psalm 139, NLT)

The feeling of disconnect from God that many of us experience is often due to our being unplugged from the present moment. When we are unplugged, we cannot experience God. As the Psalm says, there is nowhere God is not, but when we are unplugged and disconnected from the present now, we become blind and deaf to His presence. As Jesus says:

Are your hearts hardened? Do you have eyes but fail to see, and ears but fail to hear? (Mark 8:17-18, NLV)

The present is like an electrical socket. That is where the current of spiritual presence flows. Most of the time our little forked plugs are wildly waving around all over the place. Think of how a water hose gets out of control if no one is holding it as the water blasts full force. When we pray, we are making the effort to plug into the electrical socket and find the light of Christ so it can pour into and through us. Our hearts and minds are opened when we make the connection.

❧

To find a prayer phrase that is right for us, we begin by sitting quietly, relaxing our bodies, and focusing our attention on the Divine presence. We imagine that Presence as being fully present right here, right now. Turning our full awareness to Spirit, we imagine God asking us, "What do you want Me to do for you?" Answer this question for yourself. When we have an answer, we can begin to work with it to make it a prayer.

To make a prayer out of our request, we put it into a phrase of three to nine syllables. Within this phrase we place a form of the divine name that intimately connects us to Spirit. The name is the praise in our prayer, and the request is the petition. A few examples are: Christ, heal me with your love. Guide me, Spirit, to your will. Save me, Light Divine. Bring peace to my heart, Mother God.

We can put the phrase in any order and put in any words that reflect our spiritual desires. We may come up with several requests at first. We can work with these until we come to the heart of what we want and need from the Spirit. Look at the examples above for guidance. Be sure the petition is about our needs, not someone else's needs. It is our own personal request made intimately to God.

Once we have found and formed our request into a prayer of praise and petition, we can begin repeating it over and over. The prayer is the way we open our hearts and minds to God and keep ourselves aware of His presence. We are plugging into the spiritual electrical socket of the present moment. By repeating the prayer, we draw it into ourselves so that we can be praying at all times.

✍〜

The emphasis on saying a repetitive prayer all the time is an incredible gift for us householders. Our lives are deeply involved in the activity of the world. Repeating a spiritually inspiring word or phrase over and over is a portable practice. We can be standing in the bank line, sitting in a doctor's office, or stuck in freeway traffic and still be saying our prayer. We can be cooking dinner, washing dishes, sitting in a business meeting, or working on our car, and still be saying our prayer. There is really no reason not to be praying all the time—or, as St. Paul says, to "pray without ceasing." (1 Thessalonians 5:17, King James Version)

I call this kind of prayer my umbilical cord to God. No matter what I am doing, the prayer keeps me plugged in and nourished. After repeating it consciously over and over, it starts to run on its own. Our subconscious mind starts taking over and carries it along when our attention has to be focused on something else. We may even say it in our sleep, or wake up with it already going in our minds. However, it is like riding a bicycle. We have to pump the pedals to keep it going before we can coast.

❧❧

The term traditionally used for this kind of prayer is monologistic, meaning one word, although a short phrase or an image can be used. Between the fifth and eighth centuries, a form of prayer evolved called the Jesus Prayer. The Jesus Prayer is "Lord Jesus Christ, son of God, have mercy on me a sinner." It is often shortened to "Christ have mercy." Rather than being a prayer that is specific to the individual, this is a phrase that has been used by many people over a very long period of time. Such long history of use by many people gives it spiritual power. Have you ever gone to an old church, or to a site long used for spiritual practice? It has a spiritual power that even non-believers of the specific tradition can feel. There is something special about a place that has been prayed in a lot. Spiritual presence seems just a bit more eminent, present, and real in such places. They have been called thin places, where the separation between the spiritual and material worlds is minimal. The same is true of a spiritual practice that has a long history of use. There is an energy and depth that we can tap into when we use it.

Whether we make up our own prayer words or use words that have been used for centuries, the prayers help us to focus our attention on God more intently. When we do this, we are taking our desire for God and relationship with Him to a new level.

When I began practicing the Breath Prayer, a shift took place in my spiritual life. My prayer went from being like a broad-beam flashlight of general awareness of Christ in my church life, worship, and conversations with God, to a laser beam where I was looking God right in the eyes, metaphorically speaking. I continued all the other activities of prayer and worship, but now there was a growing intimacy, a quiet personal place of connection that ran under all the other ways in which I was opening to Spirit. It was a significant shift from talking to God and putting energy toward God, to listening to God.

God's primary language is silence. We tend to project our own thoughts and ideas into that silence. To connect with Divine Spirit is to let Him come to us as He is, without form, without projections, as in those moments when we are with someone we love deeply and all we want to do is hold the loved one in a silent hug. No words are necessary. Our connection with the one we love is deeper than words and cannot be expressed by words. Words would bring us back up to the surface of the relationship. Making love at its best is like this. We allow our being present with the other to express our deepest feelings of intimacy.

In order to strengthen my connection to God's silence, I would take time each day to sit still and repeat my prayer with no other distraction. Repeating the prayer kept my busy mind from drifting off into the grocery list, or the plan for the day, or a conflict I had the day before, or any number of other distracting thoughts that wanted to take my attention away from God. For most of us, this is what happens: for whatever period of time we give to being with God in this way, we spend it saying the prayer, drifting off into other thoughts, then bringing ourselves back to the prayer. The prayer then anchors us in the silence where God is present.

The words of the prayer are less important than the intention behind them. After awhile we stop playing with them, thinking about what they mean, or giving them much attention. Rather, their rhythm and intention quiet our busy minds so that they run like a brook in the background of a quiet forest glade.

The quiet forest glade is the silence beneath everything else. When I began this prayer, little by little I became more able to move into this quiet place. Of course it lasted only for a short while before my mind would have some thought, like, "Wow, I'm getting good at this." Then I would be yanked out of the quiet and back to being aware of just sitting there, my knee aching, the pressures of my life flooding back in. With the Breath Prayer, I could start again by saying the prayer.

6

Phenomena

Sometimes when we sit in quiet meditation we will have experiences that are unusual. In my journal I wrote of one such episode:

> *I am not sure that I can accurately describe what happened to me. I started meditating, feeling more centered than I had at the end of meditation at other times. Although (my dog) barked for a while, I denied responsibility so that I didn't lose that centeredness. My Breath Prayer seemed far back in my head, so as it continued I visualized a cross before me. The cross changed several times- first from a jeweled gold to a rough wood to the simple gold plate of the cross (at my church). I realized its symbolic meaning and a rush of love poured from me to it. When that happened...*

physically all I can think to describe is my head felt like it must be near the ceiling, my arms a mile long, and I didn't even have the rest of my body. Actually I felt like I had lost my head, but "I" was where a head should be—except touching or near the ceiling. My Breath Prayer started to speed up, so I slowed it down and tried to continue visualizing the cross. My eyelids fluttered; it was all I could do to keep them closed. The whole pace seemed to pick up, everything seemed fast. Then the buzzer went off.

When we sit quietly with God in prayer, listening for Him, we become more aware of our own internal state. Our senses become more alert. Phenomena can occur for which we may not have any explanation. People have reported smelling incense, hearing their name called, and seeing colored lights or images. We might find memories arising, and emotions welling up. Many people experience grief or anger flooding them without any awareness of a thought associated with it. Sometimes we suddenly get the answer to a question that has been bothering us, a certainty about a direction we should take, or inspiration for a new idea. Our experience of time becomes distorted, such that we may feel that only seconds have gone by when it is actually thirty minutes or more. Or it may go the other way, where only two minutes have gone by and we feel like it has been hours.

All these things are within us and come to our awareness because we are finally listening to our inner selves. Have you ever been somewhere that has a grand-father clock? When we are in such a place and there is a party going on, the noise and activity of the party keep us from noticing the gonging of the hours or the tick-tock of the swinging pendulum. However, as soon as the guests have left and the room is quiet, the clock suddenly seems loud and impossible to ignore, espe-cially if we are trying to sleep in that room, as I once did. Becoming aware of our internal activity is like this, as we start to quiet down in our meditation.

We may also have experiences of God during these meditations. In the following example, my husband was meditating directly in front of me. Meditating with others can enhance our awareness of God's presence.

My hand shakes now as I write. I felt relaxed as I began, and my Breath Prayer seemed both in my heart and in my mind. I allowed myself to think that I would not expect anything in particular to happen, but that I would expect or wait expec-tantly for something. As I sat, my body seemed to begin to vibrate. Every inch of my outer body seemed to. Then I felt warmth in front of me. I thought—Christ is in front of me—a warm ball of light. As I thought this, I felt a shot go through me of love and excitement and said my Breath Prayer—Fill me with your spirit, God. My body was no longer very real to me, but I became very aware of (my husband's) spirit near me. I didn't feel that our bodies really separated us. I felt closer to him than the physical distance, which my mind recalled when I had closed my eyes. I felt that Christ and (my husband) and I were all sitting in the room together. I continued my Breath Prayer, concentrating on Christ's presence, and I felt overwhelmed.

I have no doubt that God's spirit truly did fill me. I began to cry and felt myself gently float to an awareness of the physical reality around me. …I felt like I drifted back from somewhere.

Although such experiences are encouraging, we must be careful not to be sitting in order to have experiences. As I said in the journal entry above, I set out to just sit, waiting expectantly, but without expectations. This is critical in our meditation. We are there to be open to God in His silent presence. We are not there to be entertained. These experiences are like road signs on a highway. They let us know we are on the right path as far as getting quiet, settling into a deeper place within, and keeping our attention focused. However, they are as much a distraction from our true intention as a dog barking outside or a lawn mower revved up by our neighbor.

When any of these phenomena occur, we must do what we do with all distractions. We acknowledge them, let them go, and return to our prayer. We then refocus our attention to God's silent presence with us, waiting with an open heart and mind for God to come to us in whatever way He intends. This is the same attitude we must take when absolutely nothing happens in our meditation except the constant movement into thought and back to our prayer. It is not for us to determine what is a "good" period of sitting or a "bad" period of sitting. Our effort is precious to God. Just putting ourselves into the position of trying to be with Him as He is brings great benefits. In fact the slower, less interesting meditations are the very foundation for what we are able to take back out into the world with us, such as patience, humility, and letting go.

7

Enhancing Prayer

There are things we can do that enhance the likelihood of our staying focused and alert in prayer. These are things we do to help us open to God more readily. Several places in my journal entries above indicate that I was doing more than just saying my Breath Prayer. At one point, I visualized a cross. At another I imagined Christ's presence as a warm ball of light. I emphasized my prayer being in my heart as well as my mind.

Although I have made the point that our purpose is to open to God and not to be entertained, there are times when our busy minds just will not settle down. A little extra help can come in handy. These aids to our prayer are particularly helpful to us householders. Since we usually live very stimulating lives, we need all the help we can get to settle ourselves down and draw our attention back to God and away from that next thing we need to do.

A supportive environment for prayer is important. Having a place to regularly sit down with God helps to prepare us for the kind of prayer that will take us to the center of God's presence within us.

> *But when you pray, go into your room, close the door and pray to your Father, who is unseen. Then your Father, who sees what is done in secret, will reward you.* (Matthew 6:6, NIV)

In order to let go of what is happening around us, we need a sense of peaceful security. We have to be able to let go of the world's attractions and focus our attention on opening to God. Having one specific place allows us to create a sacred space where we can meet with Him without distraction. When we pray in the same place over and over, it becomes more of a thin place for us. Our minds naturally begin to adjust to the idea that when we are here in this way, we are here to be with God in prayer.

Consider using a living room chair, propping yourself up on your bed, or sitting on a cushion on the floor. We can even use a closed toilet seat if our family will leave us alone only when we are in the bathroom. I am very fortunate that my husband and I are able to dedicate a room in our home to prayer. If it is possible for us to create a space in our home that is specifically for worship and prayer, I highly encourage this. It reminds us of our priorities, but also lets our children and our friends know what is important to us.

Our space can be made more sacred by adding a few items that remind us of our intention, such as a candle, a blanket or shawl, a spiritual book, a picture, or burning incense; whatever creates a feeling of holiness and preparedness. These items can define even a very small place in our home or office as our place for prayer.

When I was in private practice, I set up an altar in my office on top of a low bookcase. It was not so obvious that it would disturb my non-religious clients, but it was a place I could turn to between sessions to center myself in God. On the bookshelf I had a sculpture, which the artist, Thomas Blackshear, named *Prayer*. It is a black man in a white robe, kneeling with his hands clasped at his chest, his fingers interlocking. His face is raised upward, but his eyes are tightly shut. He is relaxed, his legs folded beneath him, resting on his calves, bare feet peeking out from under the edge of his robe, while at the same time his body is held in alert stillness, as though he is ready at any moment to leap forward. It is the most perfect example of prayer. His whole body appears to be reaching up and outward, but his attention is concentrated in a deep interior place. It reminds me of a Zen Buddhist retreat I attended which was called *Yong Maeng Jong Jin*. I was told that in English this means *to sit like a tiger while leaping*. Even a brief glance at this sculpture reminds me to pray. It helped make my office a sacred space.

◈◈◈

Another useful item assisting us in prayer is a timer. A watch that counts down, a kitchen timer, or a special chime made for this purpose can free us to relax into our prayer without worrying that we will miss our next commitment. One person shared with me that she used a tape recorder that starts out with soothing music, which goes silent for the period of her meditation, then resumes at the end of her meditation. Figuring out what works best for us is part of the creative process in our prayer lives.

Another story I heard was of a mother of young children. She did her meditation on her kitchen floor with a brown paper bag over her head. She trained her children that as long as she was in this position with the bag, they were not to disturb her. From what I was told, it actually worked for her.

Setting aside a place and time for prayer in this concentrated way feeds our ability to take the prayer back out into our lives. This time apart strengthens the movement of the prayer so that it can more easily continue when our attention must be directed toward the demands and activities of our lives. What we experience in our time of silence, solitude, and prayer becomes a foundation within our hearts, a kind of knowing that God is present. Our hearts become a sanctuary that goes everywhere with us.

❧

The heart is often considered our spiritual center. Have you ever seen the picture of Jesus with a burning heart? The flame is the indication of the spirit alive within. St. Gregory of Sinai, a Christian desert father, instructs that we should sit in our quiet, solitary place and draw our mind into our heart. From this place within us, we are then to cry out to God, faithfully seeking Christ in our heart.

It can be quite helpful to imagine our prayer being spoken out of our heart. We can even imagine lips on our physical heart if this helps us to move the awareness of our prayer from our heads to our hearts. Activating the heart with the prayer opens us more fully to God through love and attention.

There is a story in the Bible about two disciples who were walking to Emmaus after Jesus had been crucified. They were discussing all that had happened. The resurrected Jesus joined them, but they did not recognize him. Referring to scripture, he addressed their many doubts. When they came to their village, they invited him to come eat with them. At the table he broke the bread and gave thanks, just as he did at the last supper.

Then their eyes were opened and they recognized him, and he disappeared from their sight. They asked each other "Were not our hearts burning within us while he talked with us on the road and opened the Scriptures to us?" (Luke 24:31-32, NIV)

We often make references to our hearts when we are deeply touched. Our hearts do burn when we feel something strongly. We say our hearts are broken when something severely disappoints us. We call someone warm-hearted who is kind and compassionate. We speak of heartfelt apologies. Our hearts are a place where we get in touch with what we most value, what is dear to our hearts. This aliveness of heart comes from our connection to something larger than ourselves. Often in my prayer I have experienced my heart expanding, feeling full. God's love fills our hearts to overflowing. To place our conscious prayer in this area of sacred aliveness is to quicken the connection with God at a deeper level.

❧❧❧

Visualization, like imagining we see lips on our heart, can be helpful to focus our attention and settle our minds to our intention to be present with God. St. Ignatius of Loyola taught the use of visualization in his meditation exercises. He instructs us to study various scenes in the life of Christ from the Bible and to imagine ourselves in them, taking a role and truly experiencing the situation through our imagination. We can visualize images, people, or environments. I did this in my journal entry, visualizing a cross, which I imagined in my heart. Sometimes visualization is led by someone else who verbally guides us through an experience. This can often open us to places in ourselves that have been blocked or wounded. It can help us bring the prayer into these places for healing.

Sometimes visualizations come spontaneously. Once when I was at home alone, I was sipping tea in front of my fireplace and writing in my journal. I find journaling a very meditative practice. Suddenly Jesus appeared in front of me. He was pointing forward. I went with the image, eyes closed, and could see myself fall at his feet, grasping the edge of his robe and not wanting to look where he was pointing. His eyes were full of love and compassion, but also stubborn insistence as he jabbed his finger outward. Slowly and hesitantly, I imagined myself loosening my grip on his robe and looking in the direction he demanded. To my surprise, it was a prairie-like landscape of undulating hills covered in waving golden grasses fading off into the horizon. It seemed so peaceful and beautiful. Something in me broke open, and I felt excited and peaceful at the same time. As I wrote this experience in my journal, I realized I had been afraid of some coming changes in my life, and that God was letting me know it was okay, and would even be good.

ᖇᑎᕐᐤ

Icons are images or pictures that remind us of our spiritual intention. The sculpture of the praying figure I mentioned above is an icon. There are formalized icons of Mother and Child or of Jesus. There are icons of saints. I had to experience this form of prayer before I was able to appreciate it. The church I was attending had a small chapel to the side of the larger church and sanctuary. I attended the early-morning service there because it was quiet and more meditative. Behind the altar was a huge Italian-style painting of Mary, the mother of God, and child. At that point in my life, the whole Mary thing made me uncomfortable. I now see her as a feminine face of God. Every Sunday I was on my knees before the service, saying my prayer, staring up at this dramatic picture. Often I would close my eyes to shut it out, but over time I became comfortable with the image. Then one morning as I was saying my prayer and looking up into the reds, blues, and yellows of the painting, I suddenly realized it was a picture of God.

Like so many spiritual experiences, it is hard to describe. Only after the experience can we try to put words to it. My experience was not a mental awareness at first, but a visceral one. My whole body responded, as though experiencing the picture for the first time. I just knew as I looked at that picture that I was seeing God—not Mary, not a baby, not flowing robes, not muted colors, but God. My heart beat faster and I got goose bumps. Later I could see it was a totality, the whole was greater than the sum of the parts. I could see that it was not only the visual images, but also the power of the loving relationship between the figures that represented God. The very colors glowed with God's presence. The shadowy parts of the painting were the mystery of God embedded in the rest. But, again, the thoughts and ideas to explain it came after the incredibly powerful experience of its just being God. It was less about ideas than a sensation that the veil of this world had been lifted, and my heart could see.

∽◦◡

Walking prayer is another way to enhance our prayer experience. I particularly like this one as a householder, because it serves many purposes and can be translated into ordinary life. During our meditation, where we sit still for a period of time, walking prayer is a nice way to give our bodies a break while still praying. We may sit for a long period of time and then when the timer goes off, we get up and walk slowly around our prayer space, saying our prayer, being aware and attentive to God even as we are moving, then return to our seat and continue our sitting meditation.

One of my favorite ways to do walking prayer is to take off on a mountain path or a beach. Walking without distractions, aware of the environment but lost in my prayer, I find I flush out my mind, relax my body, and become much more aware of God's presence in nature. This practice can make walking anywhere a prayerful experience. When we go to the mall, we may find ourselves having to walk long distances between stores. Walk in a mindful, prayerful way, repeating our prayer, and we are doing walking prayer while shopping. This is much easier to do when we have practiced saying our prayer in our sitting meditations.

～○～

Do you enjoy singing and dancing? **Chant** is music set to spiritually inspired words. Music and singing are loosely used in regards to chant. A chant can be made up of a single note. I have chanted "God" in this way. We draw out the word to "G-ah-ah-ah-d." It is quite powerful when done in a group where everyone finds their own pitch and tone then chants it together. There is a celestial song that the universe sings at all times to God, and when we chant, we join in this heavenly chorus. I have set my Breath Prayer to music. I find it helps to make boring tasks prayerful. While driving my car, doing housework, or sorting through old paperwork, I will chant my Breath Prayer out loud.

I have had the pleasure of participating in liturgical **dance**. Spiritually oriented music is set to choreographed dance patterns and then presented to the community. The dancers and the congregation are drawn into prayerful awareness through the movements and music. Of course, it does not have to be choreographed dance to be prayer. My husband and I were hiking in the coast range of California. By the time we got back to our car, the moon was the only light around. We went out on the cliff overlooking the ocean and danced in wild free movements full of the joy and beauty of God.

თოთ

I am particularly fond of **liturgy and ritual**. They create a structure within which I can let my prayer flow freely. Churches vary in their use of these; some try for as little as possible, others are rigidly structured. I find either extreme dissatisfying. In the Episcopal Church to which I belong, there is a structure for service and specific prayers that are used. The Eucharist, sharing of Christ's body (the bread), and His blood (the wine) take place at most services. Unfortunately, many Episcopalians get caught up reading the prayers and let the liturgy carry them along mindlessly. I encourage people to memorize the repeated liturgical prayers like the Nicene Creed, the Gloria, and the Confession. When we know these by heart, we can begin to pray them from our hearts.

When I moved to California, I had a lot of trouble finding a church with which I was comfortable. Several I visited were in conflict and crisis. Some were spiritually dead. I had been told of a woman who used to be an Episcopal nun who was now part of a Hindu ashram in the area. I checked out the ashram and began attending their services. I participated in many of their community activities and worship. They were very warm and welcoming. Many of the spiritual activities reminded me of Christian rituals and liturgy. One such ritual renewed my effort to find a Christian church.

At that particular service everyone was invited up to the front of the church to sit on the floor as Mataji, the spiritual leader of the community, handed out small pieces of a sweet cake. She moved among us popping the small morsels into our mouths. The resemblance to communion, the Eucharist, was so pronounced that my heart burned within me. I experienced such a longing of love for Christ that I knew I had to return to my own tradition. It was very soon after that someone told me about the Episcopal Church that had the icon of the Mary and Child in the small chapel.

Liturgy and ritual are not limited to church. When we come to our specific time of prayer, it can be very helpful to create our own liturgy and ritual to prepare us for our silent time. Doing some stretching or yoga, reading something spiritually oriented, lighting a candle, burning some incense, then settling into our meditation seat, doing intercessory prayer before or after, ringing a bell before and after, any of these activities can enhance our ability to transition from our active lives into our time of prayer.

⌒〜⌒

As I mentioned above, part of our ritual can be reading a spiritually inspiring work. One form of Christian prayer is called **Lectio Divina**. As the name implies, it is divine reading. There are four stages to this practice. A passage is chosen that is not too long or complicated, such as the story of the disciples walking to Emmaus when Jesus showed up that was mentioned earlier, or part of a Psalm. We are not trying to read to gain intellectual knowledge, but to open our hearts and minds to God.

The chosen passage is read once, either aloud or silently, with the intention of absorbing the words and letting them flow over and through us. Then it is read a second time, during which we listen for a word or phrase within the passage that draws our attention. It can feel like we are being guided to this word or phrase. Then the passage is read a third time, during which we allow a prayer, a response to what the reading is saying to us, to arise from our hearts to God. At this point, we are open to God. Our hearts have heard Him speak to us through the passage, and we have offered a prayerful response. The flow of communication between God and us has been opened. The passage is read one last time with the intention of deepening that connection with God that is beyond words. At that point we rest in God's presence, having moved into a deeper form of prayer called Contemplation. It is the prayer of silence and stillness, which is discussed in the next chapter.

∾◗◖∾

All of these options for prayer are tools that we can use, but the bottom line is still the opening of our hearts and minds to God. There is no right way above all other right ways. We must find what works best for us. There was once a hermit who went out to an isolated island to live in solitude, silence, and simplicity. He had been there many years. An official of the church decided it was time to visit this hermit and see how he was doing. He rowed out to the island.

The hermit greeted him with enthusiasm and invited him to sit down over a cup of tea. They spoke about how things were going then the official asked the hermit what prayer he was using. Happily, the hermit shared the prayer he had used all these years. Horrified, the official informed the hermit he was saying it all wrong and immediately told him the correct way to say the prayer. The hermit too was horrified and he thanked the official, deeply grateful.

The official, feeling quite satisfied that he had

guided the hermit to the right path, took his leave and headed back across the water in the boat. When he was far across the water, he heard the hermit anxiously calling out to him, asking for the correct form of the prayer, as he had already forgotten it. Smiling indulgently, the official turned around and to his great surprise saw the monk walking across the water toward him.

8

Contemplation

Ironically, the more we pray, the more we yearn for God. Rather than feeling satiated by our efforts, we feel our hunger more intensely. This is actually a good thing. Because of this, we become motivated to keep pursuing what is a difficult and challenging journey of the Spirit. At first our active efforts to draw closer to God are a great blessing that make us more aware and attentive. However, over time we can become dissatisfied with these. Although they bring us into awareness and attention that provide experiences of God, they can also be a distraction from the oneness we desire with God. We are experiencing our prayers, feelings, and emotions, not the One who is beyond all thoughts, feelings, and emotions.

Earlier I spoke of coming to relationship without words. When we are with someone we love, sometimes it is more meaningful and intimate to sit together in silence, holding hands, gazing into each other's eyes, and being present without words or thoughts. In the fiction book *Saint Francis* written by Nikos Kazantzakis, there is a story of two of the brothers from the monastic order coming to visit Francis. They came into the hut where he lived, kissed his hand and sat down on either side of him without saying a word. Now and then Francis would reach out and touch them, but no one spoke. Many hours passed, but they never said a word. The narrator reports that there was energy in the air among the three men as though an unspoken conversation were being shared. He suggests it is how the angels in heaven must communicate.

☙❧

Contemplation is the movement away from active prayer, into our silent gazing in loving receptivity to God. By active prayer I mean the kind of prayer where we are consciously doing something. In active prayer we use our senses, our minds, and our bodies to try to tame the busy distractions that keep us from being with God in the moment. In contemplation, we move into the silent place without any activity.

To actually reach that place of deep intimacy and silence is a gift of grace. However, we can encourage the movement toward this kind of prayer. A type of prayer has been developed called Centering Prayer. Although it is a monologistic prayer in that we still use a word, phrase, or image to remind us of our intention to be present with God, we do not repeat it over and over. Instead, we say or think it once, then sit quietly waiting in the silence. We repeat it only when we find we have drifted too far from our intention. Then again, we say or think it only once, to remind us of why we are sitting in prayer. In my meditations I will often start off with my Breath Prayer, but as I grow more quiet and still, I shift to Centering Prayer.

Fr. Thomas Keating, a Cistercian priest and monk, has taught Centering Prayer for many years. He started an organization called Contemplative Outreach, which teaches and supports the practice of Centering Prayer throughout the world. He claims that it is our natural tendency to be drawn toward the silence of God. What Centering Prayer does is give us the small tool that helps us to let go of the thoughts and distractions so that we can naturally sink into the presence of God as He is. He claims that our wills and our minds were designed to go in this direction. If nothing gets in their way, they naturally move toward this quiet inner space.

As householders, we may find this hard to believe. Our busy lives are ruled by distractions. We often feel compelled to move away from that silent presence in order to keep our world running smoothly. However, once we have tasted God's presence, the stirring of our hearts toward Him is a hunger that draws us forward.

Fr. Keating has stated that the people he knows who are the farthest along in their prayer lives are also married, or busy in the world with ministries.

Contemplation is a practice of letting go. When thoughts come, we let them go. When distractions arise, we let them go. We do not fight them or get busy with more active prayer. We let them go, and let ourselves sink naturally back into the silence of God's presence. As with all prayer that we initiate, it is a practice. We have to keep practicing. When we do, we become more available for grace to take us into the depths of intimacy with the Divine.

∽◦∾

As we move more deeply into this kind of prayer, we experience another shift. This next level of prayer can cause us some anxiety. We may feel deserted by God because all the experiences we have had of Him previously are no longer available. We may feel empty, alone, and lost. All the feelings and emotions that made us certain of God's presence are gone. When He comes to us as He is, we have no markers for confirming His presence. Now we must learn to trust at a much deeper level. We must allow God to work within us without knowing what He is doing. This brings us back to the courage, strength, and love necessary to follow this path.

Once I was on a ten-day silent meditation re-treat sponsored by Contemplative Outreach. We had been meditating and living silently in community for several days. During one of the meditation periods I began watching my breath. Normally I find this dif-ficult. I always end up trying to manage the breath rather than just watching it. My prayer was deep in the background and went silent as I watched. There was movement around me and I realized it was time for walking prayer, though I had not heard the bell rung for the end of the meditation period. Only then did I realize that a long time had passed and I was com-pletely unaware of anything.

As I have said before, these experiences are hard to describe. Rather than feeling lost and alone, I felt awed. I was not asleep. It seemed as though my mind were completely at rest in silence. As I opened my eyes, I could not believe how normal everything looked. Everything seemed brighter and clearer, but just the same. I did not feel like I had gone anywhere, but I was not sure at all where I had been. I just knew that I had gone deeper than ever before—and that deeper was right here. There had been no images, thoughts, experiences, or awareness of anything. I just knew.

When I talked with Fr. Keating about this, he simply said, "You don't need too many of those." At the time I was not sure what he meant, but I believe I do now. Contemplative prayer draws us ever closer to union with God, naked before Him and one with Him.

In those deep still places, God does His work in us beyond our awareness. We experience nothing, because our senses, our thoughts, and our self-consciousness have all been silenced in the great silence of God.

Prayer is composed of a multitude of pathways to the Divine. When we go deeply into prayer, we forge more intimate bonds with God, and He can do His clean-up work at the deepest level of our souls. Yet, we must rise from our moments of deep prayer and go back out into the world. That which is forged within us when we sit in silent communion with the Divine is what goes out into the world with us. Because of the experience of those deep moments, dancing on a moonlit ocean cliff becomes prayer, liturgy becomes prayer, and a moment of intimacy with another person becomes prayer. Those moments of silent being with God let us know that everything we do is prayer. Our being alive is prayer. We are His creatures. We are one with Him. We do not need too many of those experiences to be opened to God's reality and to take that knowledge back out into the world.

❧

Fr. Keating tells us the goal for all Christians is union with the Divine. Paramahansa Yogananda, a holy Hindu who taught in the West, tells us that the most advanced yogis live in constant union with God and are able to keep this focused awareness whether in meditation or actively engaged in the world. St. Paul says, *I have been crucified with Christ and I no longer live, but Christ lives in me.* (Galatians 2:20, NIV) In a video of Peace Pilgrim, she hesitantly shares with a friend that there was a point at which she died to self. She no longer had any selfish concerns, and fully lived the peace and spiritual freedom she taught.

This is where we are headed. Clearly, it is possible in this life. To be God's completely is something we can do. There are people who are living proof that union with God is something to be lived as a human being in normal life. We are not reaching for the impossible. We are not being set up for failure. Jesus prays:

> ...*Father, just as you are in me and I am in you. May they also be in us so that the world may believe that you have sent me. I have given them the glory that you gave me, that they may be one as we are one: I in them and you in me. May they be brought to complete unity to let the world know that you sent me and have loved them even as you have loved me.* (John 17:21-23, NIV)

We are perfect, but not complete. The artist Michelangelo is credited with saying that the way he created a statue was that he saw the statue in the stone, then just chipped away everything that was not the form. God sees us as the perfect reflections of Himself for which He made us. We are already holy in His sight. He and we together spend our lifetimes chipping away the parts that are not His form. It is our job to let go of those parts and open to the One who created us. God does not force us to change. However, He provides every opportunity for us to choose His way. At times, this can seem quite painful. Other times, it is a great relief and joy. We are never abandoned in this process, though at times it can feel like it. When God seems most distant from us, we can be sure He is actually so close that we are having trouble seeing Him. This requires trust and love, the foundations of a true relationship.

Section III
Relationship

9

Love

Relationship is the way we nurture love and manifest God in the world. As we grow toward holiness, we grow in our ability to love and to relate to others through our oneness with the Divine. We all know that relationships can be very difficult. It is in relationship that we chip away all those parts of ourselves that are not God. It is in the midst of relationship that we continually have the opportunity to choose God's way or not.

After many years in my first marriage, my husband began having affairs. Finding out about the affairs created great pain and turmoil in me. I learned of the first affair when I overheard my husband talking with a friend on the phone about the other woman. My internal reaction was anger, hurt, and a desire to either pull away or strike out. Instead, I went out into our backyard and began to pray. I knew doing this God's way was beyond my natural abilities, but I wanted very much to handle it His way. I was able to confront my husband calmly and he admitted he was in a relationship with another woman.

In my time of meditation and prayer, I would ask God to help me love the other woman. My feelings kept drifting toward anger and blame. I would take my anger and fear to God and ask that He transform it into something more in line with His will. I despised the choices my husband and his lover were making, but I refused to hold bitterness within me. I worked very hard to keep my heart open and allow God to work in and through me. By holding myself open and receptive to God's guidance in the situation, and keeping the other woman and my husband embraced in my heart, I was later able to feel at peace.

After two years of doing everything God showed me to do to try to save my marriage, God gave me the inner permission to leave. Had I allowed hatred, bitterness, and anger to shut me down, I would have been much more damaged inside myself. As it turned out, God was able to take me to new places and bless me in new ways.

∽೧෨∽

Relationships are like being placed in a rock tumbler. All the rocks we want to get shiny and smooth are thrown into the tumbler and it is turned on. The action that smoothes out the rough places on the rocks is their knocking against each other over and over as the tumbler spins. This world is our rock tumbler, and all the other people in this world are the rocks that tumble against us, bumping off the rough edges that keep us isolated and incomplete.

As householders, our lives are full of relationships. There are a lot of rocks in our tumbler: family, friends, coworkers, acquaintances, teachers, students, doctors, lawyers, accountants, pastors, policeman, grocery clerks, drivers on the road, and on and on. Each relationship provides a different set of challenges. In order to promote healthy relationships, we must constantly choose how we will be with the people in our lives.

As we strive to live our lives as Holy Householders, our dependence on God to guide us in how to do relationship becomes more evident. God wants us to relate to others as He does. The way He relates to all of creation is with love.

❧

Cynthia Bourgeault, an Episcopal priest and internationally known retreat and conference leader, teaches that this world and plane of existence are particularly precious because they are the only plane of existence in which we are able to live and experience the heart of God manifested. She makes the point that because this world is full of difficulty, loss, sadness, hurt, and heaviness, it is also the one place where compassion and mercy have the ability to show themselves in full glory and grace. She says that when we run up on the hard edge of this world, we have a choice as to how we will respond. We can choose to be bitter and angry. It is true that things in life are not fair. But it is in this world that we can also choose to manifest steadfastness, tenderness, commitment, sacrifice, giving, compassion, empathy, warm-heartedness, sweetness, and the mercy of Christ. The gifts of love are costly here, and to choose them over our personal self-righteousness is to embody Christ in a way that can be done only under these conditions.

❦

Love can make us feel good, but it also strips us naked. The more we love, the more wide open we are. Try this exercise. Think of something that upsets you. Let yourself really feel it. Now be aware of how you feel inside. For most of us the feeling will be one of tension, withdrawal, a closing down of ourselves, a tightness inside that wants to push away that which is upsetting. Now think of something or someone you love. Feel how you are inside now. For most of us there is a feeling of relaxed openness, a reaching toward that which we love, a desire to draw it closer and open ourselves to it.

When we choose love, we choose to stay open, steady, and reach out even to those people and situations that we find hurtful. Love helps us see the truth that is behind all our personal self-righteousness, and allows us to respond as Christ. In my first marriage I had to be willing to see and acknowledge the hurt and anger within me. I had to embrace my own primitive reactions. Then I had to be willing to let them go in the service of love, in the service of what I knew to be right. It left me very open to my own pain and my own need for healing. My marriage was not healed, but God's transforming love was able to do the work of healing me.

∽∾

We do not like to feel naked and exposed. We fear looking at ourselves as we are, and we fear what others might see within us. We have come to believe that there is an ugly and dark something in us that makes us vulnerable to the insecurities of life. We feel we must hide rather than bring our true self into the light. When Adam and Eve were awakened by the fruit of the knowledge of good and evil in the Garden of Eden, they became aware that they were naked. They used fig leaves to cover themselves. It was this very attempt to hide that exposed their disobedience to God.

Nothing can hide from God. God knows it all and sees it all. God is within us, around us, and in everyone else as well. Remember Psalm 139. There is nowhere that God is not. There are no secrets from God. Yet, God loves us. God still is open to us, draws us to Himself, and calls us to unite with Him. We are fully known by God and fully loved. Jesus, God incarnate, manifested Love in who and how he was when he was on earth. He showed us how to love with openness, vulnerability, and self-surrender. There is nothing false in Jesus, which is how we differ from him.

10

The False Self

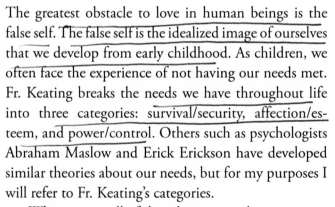

The greatest obstacle to love in human beings is the false self. The false self is the idealized image of ourselves that we develop from early childhood. As children, we often face the experience of not having our needs met. Fr. Keating breaks the needs we have throughout life into three categories: survival/security, affection/esteem, and power/control. Others such as psychologists Abraham Maslow and Erick Erickson have developed similar theories about our needs, but for my purposes I will refer to Fr. Keating's categories.

When any or all of these human needs are not met in childhood, we begin to develop patterns of thought and behavior that compensate for their absence. If a child is born into a family that does not really want him, he will feel the rejection at a very deep level. He may be too young to put words to it or understand it in any way except a feeling of fear and anxiety that he is not wanted. As infants we are totally dependent on our caretakers. Without them we would die.

Over time this child may learn that when he is funny, makes good grades in school, or dresses so that others envy him, he feels wanted and accepted. He feels more secure when he takes on these behaviors. He does not need them to survive, but at a very deep usually subconscious level he believes they are the only way he can survive, have affection, or maintain power and control. All his life he promotes these behaviors. He becomes the life of the party, the successful business-man, and the Armani-suit-wearing man-about-town who shows up in *GQ* magazine. The more success he experiences using these false self images, the more he takes them on as though they are his true self. He be-comes blind to and disconnected from who he really is.

Anything that threatens this image of him, or any time it does not work for him, he may become enraged, frightened, and aggressive. Or he may wither and with-draw, becoming confused and helpless. He may turn his anger on himself and become depressed. He has be-come dependent on his false self.

Suppose this man finds a woman who truly loves him. She sees through the façade and really wants to relate to the man she senses within him. He has some choices to make. Can he let go of his deep-seated fears about surviving, getting affection, and having control, and allow himself to become vulnerable in the face of love? Can he allow love to draw out his true self? Can he become real and open with this woman?

It all depends on how much he has grown in his life. When the false self has dominance over our lives, we tend to avoid anyone and anything that might challenge it. Most of the time we are not even aware that we have a false self, but we know what it feels like when it is threatened. It takes courage, strength, and willingness to work through the false self.

∽◦◦∾

Early in our lives we learn to ignore our own judgment and intuitive understanding of what is best for us. We learn to accept the ideas and plans that others have for us, regardless of how those plans and expectations may feel. In consequence, over the years we shut down our own inner voice and awareness. We cut ourselves off from our true self. In this shutting down, we may find ourselves doing things about which we feel some vague and uncertain shame. It is not really who we are, but it still seems required of us. After all, we really do want to survive, be loved, and have control over our lives.

One of the most hurtful but powerful experiences that can cause this shutting down is the experience of sexual, physical, or emotional abuse. When an adult or someone we respect requires that we give in to their demands for what they want from us, we may have a deep screaming need within to say, "No! Leave me alone. This is wrong." Many of us have been taught to do what we are told. As children, we often feel that we are responsible for everything that happens, especially bad things. When someone of authority says we must do or accept something that our inner intuition says is wrong, we tend to shut down the inner voice rather than protest against the person who is hurting us.

As teenagers, we are especially vulnerable to the demands of our peer group. Because we want to belong, be accepted, and survive the school years with some self-esteem, we will often ignore our inner voice that tells us what is true for us, and do things that we know are not good for us.

As adults the need to keep our false selves intact may force us to act like someone we do not really want to be. We betray ourselves often on a daily basis: ignoring a healthy diet for an indulgent one, skipping the doctor's appointment we should attend, allowing ourselves to be used by others, refusing reconciliation with someone we have hurt, or making business deals we know are shady.

The more often we shut down our inner voice, the voice of our true selves, the quieter and harder it becomes to hear. This inner voice is God's voice within us. This is the way God speaks to us, guides us, reassures us, encourages us, and draws out our true authentic self. The true self is the only self that is capable of love.

If we continue to ignore God's voice within, we become lost. Feeling lost is so uncomfortable and so similar to the feelings we had as children when our needs were not met that we begin to work even harder at strengthening our false selves. Our lives begin to feel empty and loveless. We become unable to recognize that the false self, whom we have created to answer our need to be loved, is a lie that cannot open us to love. We become caught in a trap of our own making.

∽○◯∾

In the movie *Titanic* the heroine is a young well-bred woman raised in a wealthy high society lifestyle, but she and her mother hide a secret: the family money is gone. Her father died, leaving them in debt. Her mother is insisting that she marry a very wealthy man to save the family name and provide financial security. The heroine faces a dilemma between doing what all those around her expect and doing what her heart is crying out for her to do. Her struggle is so intense that she considers suicide. She is standing on the outside of the ship railing ready to jump when the hero steps in. In the course of the movie he shows her the way to her true authentic self and a life well lived. He truly sees her and in seeing, loves her. His love strengthens her and awakens her to her own inner voice. That voice shows her that material wealth and her standing in society are not necessary for her to be loved. She listens to that voice and ends up living a life that is abundant, free, adventuresome, and authentic.

One of the best ways to heal from the false self is to develop the deep spiritual connection to God that we discussed in Sections I and II. A relationship with God can open us to our true selves and provide the love, courage, and strength that the heroine found through the hero in *Titanic*. God sees us as we are. He is eager to help us let go of the false self and become authentic. In order to have healthy relationships, in order to be capable of love, in order to become holy we need to do the work of transforming the false self into our true self.

11

The True Self

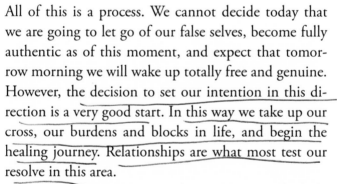

All of this is a process. We cannot decide today that we are going to let go of our false selves, become fully authentic as of this moment, and expect that tomorrow morning we will wake up totally free and genuine. However, the decision to set our intention in this direction is a very good start. In this way we take up our cross, our burdens and blocks in life, and begin the healing journey. Relationships are what most test our resolve in this area.

Once there was a man who went up on the holy mountain early in life and spent all of his time in solitude and prayer. He became very spiritually attuned, at peace, and felt himself to be one with God. One day he decided to come down from the mountain and go into the marketplace. Within a very short time, a man in the market pushed past the holy man and nearly knocked him down. The man just kept going, without a word of apology or kindness. In fact, he scowled at the holy man for being in his way. Instantly, a great rush of anger soared through the holy man's body, and he wanted to yell at the guy or punch him in the nose.

Living in solitude and doing the inner work of prayer is important in deepening our connection with God. It gives us the chance to observe and work through our false self triggers. But it is in our interactions with others that our false self is challenged. On one meditation retreat I attended with my husband, the retreatants were given the opportunity to do some physical work around the retreat facility. I chose not to do it. Others, including my husband, decided to volunteer. All of this was in silence. Suddenly, I felt an overwhelming rush of insecurity. My heart clenched with a frightened ache. I feared being left out, abandoned, and lost from the community.

I went for a walk to try to settle and understand my disturbed feelings. As I walked among the great trees of the northwest terrain, I got caught up in the beauty of alder leaves glowing like stained glass in a shower of sunlight. As I stood gazing at the beauty of it, my heart released its tense aching and relaxed into the joy of being alone with God in His silence.

About the time I had regained my inner peace, I came upon a woman who had volunteered to work; she was alone pulling weeds. I felt such a sense of relief that I had chosen to be free. I was not missing anything.

The minor distraction of feeling we have to do what anxiety seems to say is right

I realized that my fears had come from an old childhood emotion that I had not consciously experienced in a very long time. Being on retreat allowed me to stay present to myself, open my heart, and really listen to what was going on inside of me.

The pain I felt on the retreat was in direct response to relationship issues I had experienced in my life as a child. The story of the monk on the mountain coming down to the marketplace reminds us that retreat is a fine way to connect with the Divine, but living in the world is our rock tumbler. Our knocking against each other is what stimulates the process of letting go of the false self and developing the true self. The disturbances and challenges of our lives teach us what we need to change.

> *To live in the world and still maintain our inner peace, intimacy with the Divine, and love for those around us is to be truly holy. That is our work as Holy Householders: to live in the world but not of the world. We live fully engaged with the world, but we live it as Christ.*

❧

Zen Buddhism has a series of pictures that depict the process of becoming holy, or in the words of Zen, enlightened. They are called the Ten Ox Pictures. The

Ox represents the Self, our true authentic self, while the person is the Seeker in the pictures. In the first picture the Seeker is walking alone, but is looking back over his shoulder. He has a faint intuition that the Ox is present. With this first inner stirring the journey begins. In the second picture the Seeker finds a few hoof marks. These may be exposure to some teachings or an experience that hints at something more, a confirmation that the Ox exists, but is not yet seen. In the third picture the rear end of the Ox is seen while the front half is hidden behind a tree trunk. The Seeker has actually glimpsed the Ox for himself. He begins to suspect that the Self (true self) is beyond the personality self (false self). In the fourth picture the Seeker has the Ox's nose wrapped in a rope and is pulling on it. The Seeker has caught hold of the Ox and is firmly established in a practice of spiritual pursuit and discipline. This image of the Ox makes me smile. Its feet are firmly planted, resisting the pull of the rope. It is so true to how it often feels as we struggle to discipline ourselves in prayer and meditation.

The fifth picture shows the Ox meekly following the Seeker. The rope is around its nose, but it follows the Seeker without resistance. The mind is tamed and staying focused on finding the Self. The sixth picture has the Seeker riding the Ox. The mind has been mastered such that it is now an aide on the journey to Self. The seventh picture shows the Seeker in a little house looking out the window. The Ox is left outside. The

Seeker rests in the stillness of the inner places (contemplation). A large empty circle fills the eighth picture. All identity with Ox or Seeker is forgotten. The individual now rests in the True Self, beyond all thought or image. The ninth picture has neither the Ox nor Seeker, but a vague background of a willow tree and its hanging leaves, representing the merging of both Ox and Seeker into being, wholeness, the absolute Truth, oneness, God. The last picture has a much-matured Seeker returning to the marketplace, living in the world, but not of the world. This is the enlightened, realized Self. In Christian terms, the Seeker has now become one with Christ and can live in the world freely and authentically.

∽◦◦∾

The Zen Ox pictures help us recognize that being a Holy Householder is a process of seeking, finding, and becoming one with the true self. When we grow in this process, we must take what we learn back into the world and into relationships. As long as any energy from the false self remains in the other or us, we are going to find ourselves struggling in relationship. Only the true self, our Christ Self, can follow the commandment to love our neighbor as our selves. Jesus tells us the greatest commandments in Jewish law are:

'Love the Lord your God with all your heart and with all your soul and with all your mind.' This is the first and greatest commandment. And the second is like it, 'Love your neighbor as yourself.'
(Matthew 22:37-39, NIV)

These two commandments are two sides of one coin. Only in loving God are we able to love our neighbor. Only in loving our neighbor do we truly love God. Our true self is God within us. Our true self is that spark of Divinity from which we are meant to live. When we live from this heaven within, we are one with Christ, and one with all others in the world. God is everything, and everything is God. Our neighbors are our Selves. Love shows us this is true.

I often think how odd racial prejudice is. In truth we have more in common with every other human being on this planet than we do with any other species of life form. We are all bound together by our humanity. Lenedra Carroll in her book *The Architecture of All Abundance* speaks of a vision she had of life in layered webs. Each web was a different life form. The webs of animals, plants, and natural forms were all loosely woven with an exchange of energy and elements between them. The human web, however, was very tight, with very little passing through it. The nourishment and energy we all need was flowing only at a trickle within the human web, and between the human web and the others. She came to understand that we humans do not see ourselves as part of the vast larger system of the universe within which we reside. We are meant to be a major conduit for abundance, the exchange of vital energy in and between the worlds, but we are blocked—mostly by fear.

Because of that fear, we tend to lean heavily on the false self rather than opening ourselves to the true self. We are afraid of being diminished by our generosity in love. We are afraid that if we give too much away, expose ourselves too much, open ourselves too much, we will be annihilated. We could not be more wrong.

꿍

There is a fable that expresses this fear well. It is the story of the warm fuzzies and cold pricklies. There are many versions of the story, but generally it goes like this. There was a community of people who lived together in harmony, love, and peace. Every one of them had a bag in which they carried warm fuzzies. These warm fuzzies made anyone receiving one feel very good, happy, warm and fuzzy all over. People were generous with their warm fuzzies. No one ever thought about where the warm fuzzies came from or how many there were. They had always been there and available, so the people assumed they always would be.

One day a witch came to this community. She did not like all the happiness she found there. It made her grumpy and irritable. She wanted to sell her wares, but no one wanted her salves, ointments, and herbs for healing since they were all happy and healthy. She decided it was time to put a stop to it. She watched and waited until she discovered the most influential person in the community. She then began to talk with him, being friendly and pleasant. The person was very open and receptive to her. As their friendship grew, she started asking questions about the warm fuzzies: Where had they come from? How were they made? How many were there? This person had never considered these questions and at first shrugged them off, but after a while he began to wonder about it himself.

The witch began to hint that in her experience such things were bound to run out at some point, and he might want to be a little less generous about giving them away. He might use up his supply. Then what would he do? This so began to disturb the man that he stopped giving them away so freely. The witch suggested he give something less precious away, like the cold pricklies, which she just happened to know how to make. She could supply him for a price.

At first, the man would give cold pricklies away only on occasion, just to stretch his supply of warm fuzzies. Then little by little he gave fewer warm fuzzies and more cold pricklies away. Other people would feel the cold pricklies and feel confused. It made them insecure about their own warm fuzzies. The witch started selling her cold pricklies to everyone, and after a while was making quite a nice profit.

The community began to be more contentious. There were more arguments. People became more secretive. They would hoard the warm fuzzies and give them only to the people closest to them. People began to avoid each other. Pretty soon that community was a very ugly place to live. Everyone felt very bad and unhappy, which made the townspeople even more protective of the warm fuzzies they were hoarding. The witch was getting very rich.

The fable sometimes ends here, but in some versions another woman came to the community. She did not know about the witch or the cold pricklies. She started giving her warm fuzzies away freely. The adults of the town were not very receptive to this. They felt quite suspicious of her. But the children soon began following her around since she made them feel so good. Soon they were following her example, giving away warm fuzzies and making each other feel good. The adults became very disturbed and passed a law making it illegal to pass out warm fuzzies in a reckless and free manner.

12

Unconditional Love

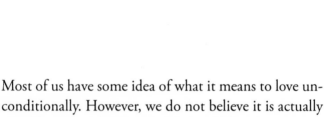

Most of us have some idea of what it means to love unconditionally. However, we do not believe it is actually possible. Even when we say that God loves us unconditionally, in the next breath we are explaining all the ways in which we have to earn it. We cannot seem to fathom the depth of love that is available to us. St. Paul tries to explain to us that grace is what has saved us. God's love is a free gift that is poured into our hearts.

> *Therefore, since we have been justified through faith, we have peace with God through our Lord Jesus Christ, through whom we have gained access by faith into this grace in which we now stand. And we rejoice in the hope of the glory of God.... And hope does not disappoint us, because God has poured out his love into our hearts by the Holy*

Spirit, whom he has given us. (Romans 5:1-2, 5, NIV)

What we misunderstand is that love breeds love. When we are loved unconditionally, as we are by the Spirit, it is a natural response to want to love in return. When we are given a precious and unexpected gift, we have a deep inner desire to give something back. It is not a demand or a requirement, but a natural response. Warm fuzzies are limitless—not because they are constructed, but because the act of giving them away creates more. Unconditional love yearns to give to the beloved what is needful for that loved one. It has no expectation or demand for itself. M. Scott Peck in his book *The Road Less Traveled* defines love as our choosing to stretch ourselves in order to support spiritual growth in others and us.

Love is manifested by a choice of our will for what is truly right and good. To be loved unconditionally is to know that the one who loves us wants our growth and spiritual abundance as much as its own. Love's generosity comes from the recognition that we are all one in the web of life and we must all grow if the whole is to come to fulfillment. When I love unconditionally, that love comes back to me through the whole. When I am a loving person, I am open to receive love.

There is a passage in the Bible that has caused all kinds of havoc in relationships, but if understood in the terms I am describing here makes perfect sense. It is the passage where the Apostle Paul says:

> *As the church submits to Christ, so you wives must submit to your husbands in everything.* (Ephesians 5:24, NLT)

It is surprising how many times in my psychotherapy practice a husband would come in with his wife and use that passage to try to convince us she should do what he wants.

What people tend to miss is that earlier in the passage Paul says:

> *And further, you will submit to one another out of reverence for Christ.* (Ephesians 5:21, NLT)

And later in the passage he says:

> *And you husbands must love your wives with the same love Christ showed the church. He gave up his life for her....* (Ephesians 5:25, NLT)

What St. Paul is describing is unconditional love between a man and a woman. When we love one another unconditionally, we want what is best for the one we love. We turn to God to hear what is true and right, and do our absolute best to understand what is right for that person and for ourselves. It is a relationship of mutual love and respect. Our false self is kept out of the interaction.

If my husband is seeking God's will and shares with me what he feels God is telling him about me, and I am seeking God's will for me, I am going to hear the ring of truth in my husband's words. Of course I will submit to them. I will submit not because my husband said them, but because I can hear God speaking through my husband and I know it to be true. It requires that both my husband and I are seeking God's will and voice, and are willing to set aside our false selves to truly hear and act on what is right.

My husband and I were living in Los Angeles. We knew that we wanted to live more simply in the mountains, but did not know where we should go. We prayed about it individually and together. Through a strange set of circumstances we were drawn to a place at the tip of the southern Sierras just two hours from Los Angeles. My husband wanted to look for work there, but I felt uncertain. God was not being clear with me about this place, and it was a really huge change.

One day my husband went by himself to the mountain town to check it out. God clearly blessed the trip. By just driving around with his intuitive faculty open my husband first found the Episcopal Church in town and spent some time in prayer there, then totally by accident came to a small medical practice that he felt called to explore. They were looking for psychologists to join their group, though they had never advertised this.

For some reason God did not speak to me directly about this move, negatively or positively, but through my husband I trusted that this is what God wanted us to do. I had to give up any false self desires about being the one to hear from God directly, and trust that God was speaking to me through my husband. Because it felt like the only right thing to do, I submitted myself to my husband's discernment. Since living there, it has become very clear to me that this was what God intended.

∝∝∝

To love unconditionally means we are willing to do what is true and right. What is true and right can be discerned only in prayer and the seeking of God's will. The false self has no place in such an equation. It is not about what we want, expect, or demand from our lives or others. It is about what we can give.

The story Jesus tells of the prodigal son (Luke 15:11-31) is an example of this kind of love. A man had two sons. The younger son asked the father for his share of the inheritance. The father agreed, and gave him his portion. Perhaps in his prayers this father had seen that this was the only chance to save his son. In love he discerned it was the right thing. How many of us would be so broad-minded? The son then took off to a distant land and blew his entire inheritance on loose living.

A famine came to that land, such that this younger son found himself in very dire straits. The only work he could get was from a local farmer who hired him to feed his pigs. For a Jew, pigs are spiritually unclean animals. This guy had sunk as low as one could go.

Suddenly the son "came to his senses," and remembering his father, decided to return home a much more humble person. He realized that even his father's servants had all the food and necessities they needed. So he decided to return, begging his father to let him serve him. His false self had not served him well at all. He was ready to let go of this and become a new man.

When the son was still a long way off, the father saw him coming. He ran to his son and embraced him, barely letting him speak his words of repentance. Then the father had his household prepare a feast to celebrate the son's return. The son had returned in ways much deeper than his physical presence. He had returned in love and humility. He was willing to give and serve, rather than just take.

The father's older son had stayed at home working with his father. This son became very upset by what he perceived as the unfairness of celebrating a wayward son when he had been such a good son and never received such a welcome or gift. The father explained to his older son, "My son, you are always with me, and everything I have is yours…. Your brother was dead and has come back to life! He was lost, but now he is found." (NIV)

This father gives unconditional love. It is not about what has been done to him or what is fair. It is about someone he loves coming out of the darkness into the light. It is about what is right being birthed out of what was wrong. Unconditional love seeks what is right in this moment, and to give generously in the service of what is best, good, and true. God does not care what we have done in the past. God does not hold grudges. God offers unconditional love and yearns for us to live out of our true selves so that we can love as He does.

The older son had not yet learned to love unconditionally. He still lived from the false self, which thinks only of itself and what it can get. Like many of us, he probably never asked for what he wanted. Often the pride of our false self keeps us from asking for what we want, for fear of becoming vulnerable. We maintain our sense of power and control by behaving in ways we feel will guarantee our needs are met. When the behaviors of the false self do not work, we get upset. The oldest son did not recognize that the saving of one soul, one person opening to the love of God and finding his true self, is cause for great joy and celebration. He did not understand that we are all united, and the birthing of a true self in one, is the birth of the True Self for us all. He had yet to experience himself as part of the whole.

13

Humility

A natural response to unconditional love is humility. Humility is a greatly misunderstood concept. We often think it means to put ourselves down, raise everyone else above us, and never acknowledge what is good about us. These are not the fruits of love. The Bible tells us:

Humility and the fear of the Lord bring wealth and honor and life. (Proverbs 22:4, NIV)

Humility is a very freeing experience. When we are humble, we are so comfortable in our own skins that we do not feel the need to compare ourselves with others. We are free of self-consciousness and insecurity. Unlike the false self—which acts out of insecurity, fear, and a sense of powerlessness—in humility we are fully secure in God. We have no reason to feel afraid. We can make choices based on what our inner voice and heart tell us is true.

If I walk into a crowded room of strangers and my false self is fully activated, I am going to be absorbed by how others perceive me. How do I look? Am I saying things well? Do I sound intelligent, smart, and funny? Are they impressed? What can they offer me? Can I make them believe I have it all together? All of my awareness is absorbed in a subconscious inner monologue, and the people around me are relevant only for how they make me feel.

Jesus went to the house of a prominent Pharisee and noticed how everyone was trying to sit in places of honor at the table. So he told this parable:

> *When someone invites you to a wedding feast, do not take the place of honor, for a person more distinguished than you may have been invited. If so, the host who invited both of you will come and say to you, 'Give this man your seat.' Then, humiliated, you will have to take the least important place. But when you are invited, take the lowest place, so that when your host comes, he will say to you, 'Friend, move up to a better place.' Then you will be honored in the presence of all your fellow guests. For everyone who exalts himself will be humbled, and he who humbles himself will be exalted.* (Luke 14:8-11, NIV)

A person coming into a party who seeks out the highest places is self-consciously aware of his position in relationship to everyone else in the room. His false self requires that he make himself appear important. Can you see how Jesus is playing to the false self? He tells the story in a way that is sure to frighten the false self of the hearers by warning of possible humiliation. The false self cannot tolerate exposure. He is challenging them to look at themselves and their behavior. He is not telling us to have low self-esteem and treat ourselves poorly. He is telling us to live humbly.

If I walk humbly into a room full of strangers, I will be living from my inner center of spiritual security. I will look out from this inner place and I will truly see the people, the way the hero in *Titanic* saw the heroine. I will be attuned to how they are feeling, what they are doing, and what is going on with them. I will be motivated by what I can contribute to the situation, because I enjoy giving. I will encourage dialogue, the back and forth sharing of thoughts, ideas, and experiences. I may listen more than I talk, not because I am insecure, but because I am truly interested in the other person. I will respond with playfulness, joy, and humor and draw that out of others. I will be open and responsive to what others bring to the interaction and encourage their participation.

My blood pressure will be even, my heart rate steady. I will feel calm, relaxed, and curious. I will be interested in my environment. My prayer will be humming gently inside of me, and I will be open to what God would have me see, understand, learn, and give in this situation.

∽◎∾

Eckhart Tolle, a counselor and spiritual teacher, tells the story of a master teacher who was the head of a monastery. A time came when a high government official in the area asked to come to the monastery for a ceremonial blessing. He arrived on the designated day with his entourage in tow. The master watched as they approached and felt a thin sheen of sweat form on the palms of his hands. After the ceremony the master stepped down from his role as the head of the monastery and went to another monastery to study and meditate.

The master recognized that his false self was still active. The sweat on his palms was a response to his insecurity about meeting with such an important personage. He knew that to be truly holy the false self has to be released. Our hearts cannot be pure and we cannot love unconditionally as long as the false self holds sway over us. Humility is in direct correlation with the false self: the more humility the less false self; the less humility the more false self.

Sweat on our palms is a pretty subtle clue to the presence of the false self. Most of us would get a lot more than sheen on the palms of our hands if we had to perform in front of someone we considered very important. Fortunately, we are called only to take our own personal next step. Remember, we are in process. We have many ways we can choose to act that help us come closer to being free from our false selves.

For example, many of us find it uncomfortable to receive a compliment. We seem to think accepting a compliment would expose how much our false self really wants it. If someone compliments us, we need to recognize it as the gift it is meant to be. We can focus our attention on the other person, rather than on how our false self feels. Do not discount that person's gift by saying, "Oh, this old thing?" Instead, honor their gift by saying, "Thank you, I appreciate your saying so." Our pleasure in the compliment is the best gift we can give in return.

∽◦◦∾

Humility is the product of unconditional love. I know God loves me. I have learned to love myself. I want to give love to others. I have nothing to fear, nothing to hide, and no need to pretend. I live with integrity; who I am on the inside is exactly how I live on the outside. My beliefs, values, and love are integrated into my behavior and interactions in the world. There is incredible freedom in living this way. I can trust that my openness to God makes me safe no matter what the circumstances. I can forget about myself and go about the business of living life to the fullest.

> *Love is patient, love is kind. It does not envy, it does not boast, it is not proud. It is not rude, it is not self-seeking, it is not easily angered, it keeps no record of wrongs. Love does not delight in evil but rejoices with the truth. It always protects, always trusts, always hopes, always perseveres.* (1 Corinthians 13:4-7, NIV)

Pure humility has no trace of the false self within it. In consequence, we see more clearly and can determine what is right for any given situation. We are not cluttered with the insecurity and fears that dominate the false self. We are able to bring love to every situation, even when that situation requires that we say no.

14

Boundaries

As we grow in humility and our ability to love unconditionally, we also grow in our ability to comprehend
what is right and what is wrong. We get better at dis-
cerning what is needful in any given situation. We
become clearer about our part in the scheme of things.
Many people and situations that confront us are just
not right. We witness events that we know are wrong.
Things are asked of us that are wrong for us. How do
we decide what to do?

As we become Holy Householders, we begin to
realize that we serve God and God's purposes, not people. We are not here on earth to serve people. Mother
Teresa of Calcutta made the point that she and the sisters were not social workers. Their work was to pick
Jesus up off the streets, to feed Jesus, and to love Jesus.

Our purpose in this life is to become God

incarnate—to live as God would live if He were a human being. This is why Jesus is such a powerful model for us. He showed us how this is done. He is God incarnate. God may call us to serve Him through people, but He is still the reason we do what we do.

When we know something is wrong, we have to be free to respond as God would respond. To know how God would respond, our hearts and minds must be open to God. We must be able to put aside the false self and to choose to act in love. We cannot allow ourselves to say yes to something that we know is not right for us just because someone else wants it. We cannot allow ourselves to say no to something when we know it is the right thing for us, even if we are afraid. We have to be willing to manage our lives God's way. This means being able to set boundaries where they are needed.

∾∾

In the Gospel of Mark (1:32-39) the story is told of Jesus going out in the early morning to pray alone. He had spent the previous evening healing people. He needed time to rest and pray. His disciples came to get him, letting him know that more people had come and were waiting to be healed. Rather than return to these people, who were certainly as deserving and in as much need as all those he had healed the day before, he told his disciples they had to go on to other towns to preach because "that is why I have come." Jesus knew his purpose was to share the good news. Time in prayer has a way of reminding us of our purpose. What God had called Jesus to do was much larger than the healing of individuals' ailments. Healing was a sideline to his mission.

Setting boundaries in our lives is essential in keeping on track with our work of becoming holy. All too often, we think we are being selfish if we say no to someone who appears to have some need or want that we could fill. This is an error in our thinking. Selfishness can arise only if we do not make the effort to discern what is right and true in God's eyes. It cares only for the needs motivated by the false self. It cares little about the cost to others or to oneself. It wants what it wants when it wants it. Selfishness occurs when we go to another person and demand from them that which may not be right for them to give. Selfishness is when someone tells us they want what they want from us and it does not matter what is right for us.

Boundaries are hard to set when we are afraid of disappointing someone. We may be uncomfortable with confrontations. We fear looking mean or stingy. Because of our fears, we tend to set boundaries in awkward and sometimes hurtful ways. We may avoid the person in order to avoid the confrontation. We may hint at our boundary, then get angry and aggressive, feeling justified because the person did not get our hint and back off. Worse still, we may not set the boundary and find ourselves doing something that we resent or have to get out of afterward because it is so wrong for us.

We are in process. Learning to set boundaries well goes hand in hand with the development of humility and unconditional love. As we grow more certain of God's voice within us, as we grow more confident in what is right and good for us, we will get better at approaching others with love and respect even when we know our choices will displease them.

❧

I was standing in the foyer of the church I was attending when the pastor's wife eagerly walked up to me and asked, "Would you be willing to work with the children in our Sunday school? It would just be a couple of times a month."

I looked her in the eye and calmly answered, "No, that is not one of my gifts. But I appreciate your thinking of me."

She stood a moment staring blankly at me; then with a somewhat confused mumble, she excused herself and moved on.

At that time, I had already considered and prayed about what I had to offer my church community. I knew that there were other ministries to which I am far more suited. Had I been uncertain, I might have let her know I would need time to think and pray about it before giving her an answer. This is one of the best ways for us to respond when we are not sure of something. We need to allow ourselves time to go to God in prayer, to listen to our hearts, and discern what is right. This also allows us a chance to practice how to set the boundary appropriately or to ask for guidance from someone we respect.

◆

Setting a boundary appropriately requires that we keep our hearts open and receptive. We have to be willing to stay present with people, aware of them, attuned to their needs, and to truly listen to what they have to say. This attitude makes it clear that we understand what they are asking and what they want. We see them, understand, and even care about them, yet we still make our decision based on what our hearts are telling us is right in the situation. It is hard for them to argue against our boundary when we show love in how we behave.

This is how Mahatma Gandhi was with the British. He was calm, listened intently, remained respectful, but still did what he felt was right and refused to do anything he believed was wrong. He held steady, stayed centered in his spiritual self, and acted in ways that exposed the wrongness of how the British were trying to rule his country. He kept himself in a place of loving peace even when pushing against British rules.

Peace Pilgrim tells of a disturbed young man with whom she took a hike. He had a history of beating his mother. On the hike a storm came up that triggered his behavior and he began hitting Peace Pilgrim.

> *But even while he was hitting me I could only feel the deepest compassion toward him. How terrible to be so psychologically sick that you would be able to hit a defenseless old woman! I bathed his hatred with love even while he hit me. As a result the hitting stopped.... The delayed reaction, because of his disturbance, had reached the good in him. Oh, it's there—no matter how deeply it is buried—and he experienced remorse and complete self-condemnation. What are a few bruises on my body in comparison with the transformation of a human life? (Peace Pilgrim Her Life and Works in Her Own Words)*

It can be hard to maintain a loving stance when faced with someone we feel is wrong or doing something wrong. However, if our boundaries are to be set God's way, they must be done with love. Remember Scott Peck's definition of love: our will to extend ourselves for the spiritual growth of another or ourselves. Setting an appropriate boundary is a way to love another person and ourselves. We are working to bring what is right into our interactions with others. We are trying to correct what is wrong in our world.

I was helped with being able to approach others with love by a sermon I once heard. In it, the priest encouraged us to recognize that we may not be able to find God in others, but we can recognize that all people are in God. This subtle shift was very freeing for me. I find it hard to see God in the heart of someone I do not like. However, it is easy to recognize that we are all in this together. We are all in God, loved by God, and created by God. We are brothers and sisters. For me to love God is to love what God loves. We are back to the web of life and the axiom to love God with all our hearts, and our neighbors as ourselves.

This kind of love does not require that we feel warm and fuzzy toward everyone. It does require that we choose to give warm fuzzies rather than cold pricklies. It means we choose to act in a loving way, keeping our hearts and minds open to others as well as to God. Our boundary-setting will be a loving act when our hearts are channeling God.

15

Communication

My husband and I were visiting his parents in Washington State. His father was driving us to dinner. His mother was in the front seat and we were in the back seat. His parents started having a conversation in which they both became tense and frustrated. My husband and I listened for a while, then turned to each other with lifted eyebrows and a shake of our heads. His parents were talking about two completely different things, yet neither of them had a clue. From their own perspectives, they each felt very right about what they were saying, and they were right. They could not resolve their differences because they were talking about two different things. We wisely chose not to interfere. Eventually, they gave up and quit discussing it, but it took awhile for the tension to go away.

Communicating is one of the hardest tasks we

undertake in relationship. The most significant reason for this is that we do not listen. That tricky false self is usually at the core of this problem. We become so wrapped up in making our point and wanting to be understood that we do not take the time to open, and receive what the other person is trying to communicate. We seem to fear that if we listen, it will be taken for agreement. We think if the other person would just listen to us, they would have to agree. Worse still, if we actually listened, we might find out we are wrong. Like so many aspects of the false self, this is a lie. We are not diminished when we listen.

When we approach others with humility and love we want to understand where they are coming from, what they mean, and what they intend. When we no longer feel threatened by the differences between us, there is no reason to feel defensive. We are eager to listen to the other person and understand what is really going on in a situation. Only then can we determine what is right and true. Only then can we become clear on what we have to give that will serve God's purposes.

そのの

The St. Francis prayer is about this shift in our behavior from being focused on ourselves to focusing on the other person.

Lord, make me an instrument of your peace. Where there is hatred, let me sow love. Where there is injury, pardon. Where there is doubt, faith. Where there is despair, hope. Where there is darkness light. Where there is sadness, joy. Oh, Divine Master, grant that I might not so much seek to be consoled as to console, to be understood as to understand, to be loved as to love. For it is in giving that we receive. It is in pardoning that we are pardoned. It is in dying, that we are born to eternal life.

When we approach others it is good to keep this in mind. In giving *of* ourselves, we in fact are giving *to* ourselves. The flow in the web of life is more abundant and continuous when we resist the urge to shut down and withhold rather than stay open and give. When we work to understand more than to be understood, we are going to be able to act more appropriately. When we interact with others we can listen intently, ask questions for further understanding, and paraphrase what we have understood to be sure it is what the other person meant. When we feel we have truly understood what the other person is trying to communicate, we can then choose whether we agree or not. With all the facts and meanings clarified, we are in a much better place to determine where we stand.

If we disagree we can attempt to explain why, but if the other person refuses to listen, do not try to force them to understand. Our responsibility is in deciding how we will behave, rather than in influencing what the other person believes. We simply set the boundary on what we are willing to do and what we are not willing to do. We can remain loving and kind, while continuing to disagree. We can agree to disagree even if the other person does not. If we get caught up in the need to have the other person understand us, we lose our power. The false self would tell us we have to win and get the other person on our side in order to have power, but that is a lie. We have no power over another person. Our power is in the freedom to act in the way we know is right for us.

∽◌◞

We have only to consider children to see this is true. We cannot make our children do what we want them to do. With teenagers this is especially clear. All we can do is influence them by what we are willing or not willing to do. The better our relationship with our children, the more likely they are to cooperate with us. The more respectful communication, love, and pleasurable interactions we have with them, the more likely they are to return these behaviors to us. On the other hand, when we see our children doing something we know to be hurtful to them, we have a responsibility to intervene.

Screaming and yelling at our children is not a good intervention, nor is it effective communication. It only alienates them further. That reaction is all about us. We are upset because the situation is not what we think it should be. Our false self is having a temper tantrum. As with all relationships, we need to be willing to listen both to the person with whom we are interacting, and to our hearts to know what the right course of action might be.

We have a lot of influence over our children based on what they want from us. Keeping our attitude kind, loving, but firm, we manage their access to their friends, the use of the car, and the new toys they want. We encourage them, listen to them, acknowledge their desires, and then make an informed decision about what we are willing and not willing to do for the good of the situation. If we are unsure, we do well to seek advice from wise counselors. For most of us, parenting well requires practice and thoughtful effort.

Children want to be heard, respected, and taken into account, just like we do. They want to be loved. By the time they are teenagers their false self is already in place. Our behavior toward them is a chance to model unconditional love and humility in their true sense. Both require being self-disciplined in following what God speaks to us in our hearts, and doing what is right. When we are committed to our path of holiness, we have a responsibility to manage our own false self and not allow it to interfere with our relationships.

Your spouse walks in the door at the end of the day with a scowl on her face, her fists clenched, and her eyes beaming hostility. You tentatively ask, "What's wrong?" Her curt response is "Nothing." What do you believe? Are you going to accept that there is nothing wrong?

As we tune into people around us, we have a tendency to believe their nonverbal communication more than we believe their words. It is harder for people to hide or distort behavioral clues than it is to manipulate verbal presentation.

This takes us back to integrity and humility. When the false self is in charge, we want to hide our inner experience. We do not want others to know what is really inside of us, for fear it will be unacceptable or make us vulnerable. We often do not want to know ourselves what is inside of us. If we can pretend everything is okay, maybe it will be.

Making the effort to be Holy Householders means we are taking the time to get to know ourselves, accept ourselves, love ourselves, and free ourselves from the false self. When we are at peace within ourselves, we can admit we are angry when we are angry, and trust that we will take care of ourselves appropriately. When we are listening to our inner voice and spirit, our outer physical responses align with what we are experiencing internally. When the false self is in control, we may well feel one way and try very hard to act another.

Our nonverbal language can be a very helpful tool

in getting to know ourselves better. If someone comments that we just rolled our eyes, or our tone seemed a little sad, there is no reason to become defensive and deny it. Listen to what was said, and consider it. Going into our hearts and checking it out may well inform us of something that we need to address.

In the case of the spouse described above, it is a good idea to be compassionate. If someone is resistant about sharing their true feelings, give them the space they need to deal with this in their own way. When it is an important relationship like this one, we can approach the subject again later when they are feeling better, and encourage a discussion that allows us to connect with them more intimately. This does not need to become about us. Focus on the other, and on what we may be able to give to the situation that is healing and positive. This means listening to them and giving them our full attention. Even if the person is angry with us, it is better to stay open and loving and to invite honest communication so that the problems can be addressed productively.

If we act out of anger, we are more likely to get defensive anger back. If we act in a loving manner, we are more likely to get open, honest communication that nurtures loving behavior in the other. Even if the other person refuses to communicate honestly with us, we have remained people of God in our behavior, and can be at peace. If they do refuse to work with us, we will have to deal with the fact that there are bigger problems in the relationship that need to be addressed.

COMMUNICATION

⁓∽∾⁓

As we grow into our holiness as householders, we will begin to see the fruits of our efforts. It is pure delight when we find other people who are also invested in truly listening and understanding. When everyone is willing to have integrity, be truthful, and seek what is right, that is when real dialogue occurs. Dialogue is fun. Each person contributes an idea that builds on the previous idea until the conversation feels like a creative exploration mutually shared.

When everyone is working to communicate effectively, problems get solved, satisfactory compromises are reached, and everyone walks away feeling heard, respected, and cared for. Trust is built. Intimacy develops. There is greater willingness to work on problems together in the future. Warm fuzzies are spread all around. We experience love.

16

Community

In my early years I was raised in a family of women. Because my father was an Air Force pilot he was gone weeks at a time. My brother was not born until I was twelve years old. So for a long time it was my mother, two older sisters, and I who lived together. Saturday mornings we each had a household task and did housework together. I remember my mother sitting on her bed with my sisters and I spread around her, listening while she read *Charlotte's Web*. She would take us on adventures in the new locations to which we moved, often getting lost on purpose so we could discover new territory. I was reprimanded when I acted out my childish frustrations, and embraced when I acted in love. We formed a community of four. This community provided me with a sense of belonging. I knew my place in the scheme of things. I had a part to play, a way to contribute. There was security in the repeated patterns of life together.

The heart of any community is to support and encourage its members to grow and evolve. Though we may frame our experience as serving the community and its goals, in truth we are serving our need for belonging, security, meaning, purpose, and a place in the world. We are seeking to become more whole, complete, and holy. We are satisfying our hunger to be part of something bigger than ourselves. Communities challenge us as we bump up against the false self of those around us. At the same time they provide the support, encouragement, and love we need to do the hard work of becoming God's people. If our community does not serve this purpose for us, we may need to leave it and find another that will.

∽○∾

Communities tend to fall within a range from enmeshed to disengaged. This is particularly apparent in families. Either extreme is unhealthy. An enmeshed family does not allow its members to have individuality, privacy, or development apart from the whole. Families at this end have no secrets from each other. Susie and Joe have a fight, aunt Lucy hears about it, within the day everyone else in the family knows. Mike graduates from high school and enlists in the Army without consulting his family. They go into warp drive trying to intervene and stop him. This end of the spectrum can be smothering. Spiritual communities at this end of the spectrum are called cults.

At the other end is the disengaged family. In this situation the members are only loosely connected. No one knows what anyone else is doing. There is little support, encouragement, or exchange of love. There are no boundaries or rules. The members are left on their own. This end of the spectrum feels like no community at all.

Brother David Steindl-Rast, a monk, writer, and speaker trained in psychology, writes in his book *A Listening Heart* about the need all communities have to find the balance between solitude and togetherness. He makes the point that both of these are required to be healthy. He explains that if a community does not have togetherness, it breaks apart, going in different directions. If there is not solitude the community becomes an undefined mass, or crowd.

If we have only solitude we become isolated, lost from the greater web of which we are a part. Like the monk who lived on the mountain, then got upset in the marketplace, we can get lost in our own inner world and not realize what we have yet to learn. We may not learn the lessons of love.

If we have only togetherness, we begin to live side by side rather than have true connection. We lose our sense of identity and feel ourselves lost in the crowd. We need to be connected with God and ourselves through solitude to be able to connect with others in togetherness.

We all have varying needs in regard to how much solitude and community we require for our spiritual growth. Those needs may vary at different times in our lives, but we are likely to lean more toward one or the other. Finding a community that can accommodate the needs of its members is important in our being able to grow and evolve within that community. Within families, it is important to balance each person's needs with the needs of the whole.

⚬⚬⚬

All communities need some ideal or purpose that holds them together. It is the mutual interest and investment in this purpose or idea that bonds the members and keeps them and the community growing. "Grow or die" applies to communities. Unfortunately, many communities get self-absorbed and forget their greater purpose. They get caught in internal workings and politics so that they lose their way. Leadership in communities often becomes misguided, thinking that the members of the community are there to serve the leader's vision or idea of what should happen. Leaders need to remember that they are first and foremost servants of the community and the community's purpose.

All communities, not just spiritual ones, require

leadership that keeps them focused on their purpose and supports the growth and evolution of their members. When I worked at the prison, I had the distinct impression that the leadership had lost touch with its reason for being there. In that scenario, the clinical staff became trained monkeys and the inmates were widgets. Leadership pushed on the clinicians to make their paperwork look good, whether or not we were actually offering any clinically valuable treatment. Computer numbers and statistics were more important than what was actually happening. It seemed as though the administrative leadership viewed inmates not as people needing rehabilitation, but as the commodity that made the computer statistics possible.

The California prison system calls itself the California Department of Corrections and Rehabilitation. This may have been its purpose somewhere along the line, but by the time I left it was more about leadership vying for position and money. Politics and budget concerns dominated the policies and procedures. With the leadership so focused on their personal concerns rather than the functioning of the prison, the system was—and likely still is—in crisis.

Jesus expressed the idea of leadership as service by washing his disciples' feet and encouraging them to also serve those they lead. (John 13:1-17)The *Tao Te Ching* (#17) poetically tells us that in ancient times when a true leader governed, the people barely knew he was around. He did not talk about what he was going to do. He just did it. What he did was so well done; the people believed they did it themselves.

When we become leaders in our communities we have a greater responsibility to act with humility, unconditional love, and prayerful guidance from God. We are called to listen more than speak, set boundaries where appropriate, and model holy behavior seeking what is right and good for all. It is our job to keep our community focused on its true purpose and to encourage its growth and development. Leadership is an opportunity for us householders to practice the skills we are learning. We should seek out these opportunities as we grow. The world desperately needs our holiness.

❧

Buddhists have what they call the Triple Gem or the Threefold Refuge. It is like a tripod of stability for anyone on the Way. The three legs are the Buddha, Dharma, and Sangha. As I understand it, the Buddha is more than the one man who first became fully enlightened. It means Fully Enlightened One or Awakened One, and is the title used for anyone who has attained full enlightenment. The Buddha embodies the path leading to the end of suffering. It is different from Christianity, in that there is not a personal relationship with the first Buddha of ancient history, but there is similarity in that we are working to become one with Christ, as Buddhists are working to become Buddhas.

The second leg of the tripod, the Dharma, is the Buddha's teachings, and the third is the Sangha, or community. The Dharma is the way we walk the path. It is like a toolbox to liberation. The Sangha is the community of all those who have become enlightened, and it is also our traveling companions on the Way.

This Triple Gem of Buddhist teaching is a wonderful expression of what is needed for the spiritual journey. We all need those who show us it is possible to fulfill our spiritual aspirations and how that looks. We need the teachings that show us how to live day to day, and how to apply guidelines and instructions to our lives that assure us of reaching the elusive place of union, completion, wholeness, and enlightenment. We also need a community of others who can inspire, encourage, and support us on our journey to our true selves.

Section IV
Work

17

Prayer at Work

How can we be Holy Householders at work? First and foremost we must keep up our prayer life and our connection with God. The prayers we discussed in Section II are very helpful here. Repeating a prayer phrase will help keep our awareness of God alive within our subconscious when our conscious minds must be focused on the tasks in front of us. When we have decisions to make at work, the ongoing prayer can remind us to listen to our hearts and try to discern what the best choice is. It reminds us that we are working with people who are also God's children. The prayer teaches us patience, humility, and thoughtfulness. All of these are important in our work.

Buddhists teach mindfulness, which is about being fully present and aware in each moment. If we are engaged in conversation, we are fully present, paying attention to the person or people with whom we are talking. We are not thinking about the next project or meeting we must get to. If we are focused on a project or activity, we are fully present to that project or activity. We get into the flow, often losing track of ourselves and the time, because we are fully absorbed in what we are doing.

Our hearts, having been trained by prayer to stay aware of God, can be aware of His presence in whatever we are doing by being fully present. God exists only in the present moment, so when we are fully present, we are in God's presence. As we work in this way, we stop saying prayers and become prayer. We are Holy Householders at work.

⌒∽⌒

When I was doing full-time private practice I had the great benefit of working with a group that advertised as Christian therapists. Consequently, many of my clients were interested in integrating spirituality into the therapeutic work. We would often pray together. I was able to bring in spiritual examples from Scripture to enhance their understanding of the work we were doing.

On my office wall I had the picture by Thomas Blackshear called *Forgiven*. It is a picture of Jesus holding a man in his arms. The man is in jeans and a tee shirt, hanging limply, unable to stand on his own, with a look of agony on his face. In one hand the man holds a mallet; in the other a spike. Jesus is standing behind him holding him up with one arm around his middle and the other under his arm. Jesus' face is bowed over the man's shoulder as though praying while he holds him close and secure. I often gazed at this picture. When my next client arrived I would imagine that Jesus was holding that person just like the man in the picture. I envisioned Jesus sitting in the chair or on the couch holding the client in his arms and looking to me to assist him in the care of this human being whom Jesus loves.

⁓◦◦⁓

Finding ways to support our intention to bring God into the workplace will help us bring that intention into our actions as we work. At the prison I had a shiny black tile on which my husband had engraved words by Gerhard Terteegen, a Protestant religious writer of the 1700s, that helped me remember to stay calm, focused, and tranquil so that I could be a mirror of God's peace in the world. The prison was insanely busy and chaotic. Reading the words on the tile reminded me to say my prayer, breathe deeply, and calm my heart, which was often racing and stressed.

Seeking out others at work who share our interests can provide a supportive community. Praying together makes people more willing to work together God's way, even when the relationships are challenging. It is surprising how people calm and focus when prayer is brought into the work they are doing together.

I know this path is not followed by large numbers of people and it can be difficult to find like-minded colleagues. As I mentioned before, there were other people at the prison who wanted to bring light to that dark place, but we were spread out and overworked, so we rarely talked together of the Spirit. However, with my tile advertising my spiritual interests, and my way of being in that place, people did at times share spiritual ideas and come to me for spiritual support.

⋯⋯

Many of us commute alone to work. Driving alone in a car provides an excellent opportunity to pray, listen to a teaching CD, sing, chant, or think deeply. My husband used to ride the bus to his work. He would read the Bible and pray on the bus. Often people on the bus would start up spiritually oriented conversations with him. When we take advantage of this time to connect with God and His people, we reach our workplace with our hearts opened, our thoughts deepened, and God very present.

Throughout the day at work, take a few minutes to go off alone and reconnect with the Spirit. Go to the bathroom, go for a walk, or pause at your desk. When I was a waitress, I would go to a storage room. Wherever you go, take a deep breath, relax, and let God in.

18

Our Lives Are Our Work

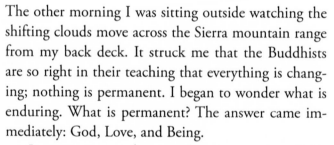

The other morning I was sitting outside watching the shifting clouds move across the Sierra mountain range from my back deck. It struck me that the Buddhists are so right in their teaching that everything is changing; nothing is permanent. I began to wonder what is enduring. What is permanent? The answer came immediately: God, Love, and Being.

It seems to me the ever-changing nature of this world is beautifully formed to help us realize it is not what we do in the world that matters as much as *who* we are as we do it. Our choices determine if we will use the material of this world to teach us, help us to grow, and to fulfill our potential. The work we choose is significant in that it reflects who we think we are and what we choose to be in the world. It is the canvas on which we paint our lives and live our being. It is the place where we offer ourselves to the world, for good or ill.

In our ignorance we often feel victim to our own choices. Our false self is often a harsh dictator forcing us into work and behaviors we do not really want. We are enslaved rather than free.

St. Paul says:

> *I don't understand myself at all, for I really want to do what is right, but I don't do it. Instead, I do the very thing I hate. I know perfectly well that what I am doing is wrong, and my bad conscience shows that I agree that the law is good. But I can't help myself, because it is sin inside of me that makes me do these evil things.* (Romans 7:15-17, NLT)

Free will means we have choice. Unfortunately, many of us are unsure of what the right choice is. We have lived in the shadow of our own needs and insecurities too long. The truth is that *our lives are our work.* To work toward the fulfillment of our true self, and living out its purpose in the world, is the only real work we have in this life. The labor we offer the world needs to be in the service of this purpose.

The day-to-day experiences of our lives are where we fulfill the work of our true selves. Our moment-to-moment choices, the goals we set, the relationships we nurture, and the jobs we choose, all show us who we are and where we are headed. The skills for finding our way are honed and strengthened in this day-to-day process. Our efforts are often called practice. In the highly trained work of the medical field they call what professionals do practice. Our spiritual work is a practice. Learning to choose well with what information we have is a process of trial and error. It takes practice. Like an artist trying to sculpt, we must be very open, willing to listen to our inner guidance, and to take the necessary risks to bring forth beauty out of the raw clay of our lives.

My husband and I have read the books and periodically watch the movie version of Tolkein's story *The Lord of the Rings*. There are many wise and moving moments in this story. One in particular stands out. Frodo, the hero, is sharing with Gandalf, the wizard, how he wishes he did not have to go through the difficult experiences he is having. Gandalf wisely tells him that no one who lives through such perilous situations wants to do so. However, all Frodo has to do is decide what he will do with the time he is given.

This is the truth for householders and hermits alike. It is for us to choose what we will do with the time that is given us. Most of our choices are not in the arena of great world-shattering change. Rather, our moment-to-moment choices shape both our world and us. It is in this present moment that we can hear the voice of God, the call in our hearts, the clarity of understanding, and know what is the right way for us. Even those people we credit with doing great things in the world had to make one choice at a time. They often had no idea where their choices would ultimately lead them.

∽◈∾

We householders give a lot of our energy and thought to our work; whether we work for an organization, our own business, or at home. It is second only to relationships, which are woven into every aspect of our lives. As we grow in holiness, we are called to ask the difficult questions that confront the choices we have made up to this point. Does our work fit our values? Does our work give us back as much as we give to it? Are we attached to our work for the wrong reasons? What sacrifices are we willing to make to do the work we truly feel called to do? What are our passions? What are our gifts? Are these being addressed in our work? If not, are we using them in another area of our lives? What is our purpose? What is God calling us to do?

W. D. Wattles in his book *The Science of Being Great* makes the point that many people avoid thinking because it is hard and exhausting to do. He explains that the impulse to think was planted in us by God. It is a natural part of our being. In order to avoid it we tend to keep ourselves busy with activities that distract us from having to think. A lot of our free time is given over to running away from our own thinking.

This returns us to the issue of courage and strength in becoming Holy Householders. It can be very scary to look directly at our lives and honestly assess if they are aligned with what we experience God calling us to do. It may require significant changes. We may have to let go of things or people that we feel are important in order to be able to embrace what is right for us, and ultimately more fulfilling.

Fr. Keating tells a story about the way hunters in Africa catch monkeys. Hunters put a sliced coconut with a sweetmeat stuffed inside into a box whose only opening is just big enough for a monkey's hand. The monkey comes along, tempted by the sweetmeat in the coconut, reaches in and grabs the coconut, but cannot pull it out of the small hole. All the monkey has to do is let go of the coconut so he can pull his hand out and he will be free. But the hunters catch the monkey because the monkey does not want to let go of its prize, and is therefore trapped.

At the prison, I knew many people who hated their jobs. Their physical and mental health was clearly being negatively affected, but they could not let go. The state offers an excellent salary, benefits, and retirement. More importantly, these people were living right up to and sometimes beyond their means. Rather than consider a job change, they would buy more toys. A new car, a boat, and an RV were the compensations for being stuck. They were the coconuts that kept them trapped. These things may have kept their families and themselves entertained, and allowed them to avoid thinking too much about how miserable they were at work, but they also kept them in debt.

As we begin to align our lives with our values and God's intentions for us, we will need to think and act on the questions I posed above. We may have to simplify our lives in order to be able to have more choice about what work we do. We may have to make paying off debt a priority. We may need to explore and research options. We may need to go to workshops and read books that help us find what most calls to us. Talking with those who are in the areas of our interests can help us network and consider what is possible. We will definitely need to turn to prayer to let our hearts guide us in the right directions.

19

Discernment and Intuition

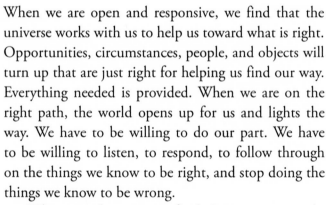

When we are open and responsive, we find that the universe works with us to help us toward what is right. Opportunities, circumstances, people, and objects will turn up that are just right for helping us find our way. Everything needed is provided. When we are on the right path, the world opens up for us and lights the way. We have to be willing to do our part. We have to be willing to listen, to respond, to follow through on the things we know to be right, and stop doing the things we know to be wrong.

When my divorce was final, I was twenty-eight years old, without children or debt. The world was wide open for me. I felt great anticipation over what God would do with me. Over a little time, my choices narrowed to two very attractive options. One was to go to graduate school and become a licensed clinical psychologist, which I believed would make me the best spiritual director I could be. The other was to go to India and live in Bede Griffiths' ashram, a Christian community blended with Hindu (Vedanta) teachings. In that direction I believed I would experience a deepening of spiritual growth that would then lead me to wherever God wanted me to go next.

I was pleased with both options and opened my heart and mind, listening for God's guidance as to which one I should pursue. Little by little a sense of clarity came where the idea of graduate school seemed to have a warm bright light around it and the move to India receded into a more shadowed and gray area within me. I experienced this as my answer, so I began applying myself toward finding a graduate school.

As confirmation of my choice, God opened doorways, introducing me to people who directed me toward a graduate program in California. I had always wanted to return to California, so I was excited by this plan. The therapist I was seeing at that time had her own therapist, who happened to be moving to the same area as the school I was considering. He did not charge me because he was not yet licensed in California when we began working together. He also had a heart for graduate students.

The place I found to live in Los Angeles was not advertised. I was driving around on a weekend visit to find a place to live. I had limited funds for this endeavor, so needed to find something quickly. As I was driving around a neighborhood becoming frustrated and anxious, I stopped in the road and prayed. Maps were spread across the passenger's seat of my rental car in great disarray.

An older gentleman was walking along the sidewalk and I felt inspired to ask him if he knew of any place for rent in the area. He glanced at the maps on the seat beside me and invited me to follow his car to a place he knew. I figured if the neighborhood looked bad, I would just keep going. Instead, I ended up renting his garage apartment for over six years. He and his wife took me in like a daughter, including me in family holidays, giving me tickets to Hollywood shows, and introducing me to a slew of unusual and fascinating people. I went to Los Angeles knowing absolutely no one, and in a very brief time had a little community of people who provided kindness and support.

༄

There have been a large number of books that speak to us of our ability to think our way into whatever we want. Some of these books give the impression that we are fully responsible for whatever is happening in our lives. We are the masters of our universe, and all we have to do is manage our thinking and everything we ever desired will be ours. I find these ideas rather disturbing. I do not want to be the master of my universe.

I would be sure to screw things up. Nor do I like the unhelpful implication that if people are living painful lives, it is their lack of control and poor thinking that got them there.

What I do believe is expressed very well by Shakti Gawain in her book *Living in the Light*. She speaks of how she had always tried to control her life by figuring out what she wanted and setting goals. Then she started practicing surrender. She found that it was ultimately not that different. The universe tended to want her to have what she wanted and it was more effective at guiding her on how to create it. She practiced becoming receptive to her intuition and acting on it even when she was not sure why she was doing what she felt guided to do. Her process is to let go of control, surrender, and leave the higher power in charge.

❦

Surrendering to God does not mean we become passive and wait around for God to do all the work. Human beings are set up with a system for good decision-making. This system is a three-way process of discernment. The three parts of this system are the emotions, the mind, and the heart. The emotions are the red flags of our system. They alert us to be aware, be alert, and pay attention. They let us know that something is going on, and we need to focus our attention on what is happening. The mind brings thought and logic to the emotional warning system. It reviews and assesses the environment, the facts, and starts processing what scenarios are possible. The heart is the center and key to the system. As I have explained before, our hearts are the place where God speaks to us. The heart guides our responses so that they reflect God's intentions. Intuition and discernment reside in the heart.

The ideal is to make choices based on a balance between these three processes. All too often we give more energy and attention to one or two and neglect the others. When this happens, our choices become distorted. When our emotions are given control, we become reactive. Our reactions can be extreme and out of alignment with the reality around us. For example, if we are trying to decide what career path to choose and we find that two different options have presented themselves, we may begin to torment ourselves with anxiety. We begin to have panic attacks, get testy with the people in our lives, and become paralyzed, unable to pursue either one. The red flag of the emotions helpfully lets us know something important needs to be decided, but we are overreacting to the dilemma.

The mind is useful for information-gathering, organizing information, and strategizing. However, when the mind takes charge of the process, it has the attitude that the end justifies the means. The mind wants to take care of business, and make things happen. It cares very little for consequences or relationships. It has a great deal of power over us. It can create scenarios and stories from the data it gathers, which can then escalate the emotions into frenzy.

Let us say for example that we are considering two job opportunities, one of which is commission-driven, and the other offers a salary. The mind begins to consider how to make the most money securely. It may even come up with unscrupulous ways to manipulate the system so the commission can be higher than the salary. It can also consider disastrous scenarios if either job is at risk of not providing enough money. The emotions react to these scenarios either positively or negatively depending on what our mind is telling us. The mind might get fixated on a thought such as "No job is ever going to make me enough money."

The heart is intended to be the guiding factor in this process. From the heart we consider God's way, our true path. We manage the emotions with love and confidence. We direct the mind toward what is ethical and right. The heart needs the input from our emotions and our minds to be fully informed and to consider what directions are available. At the same time, it listens for God's voice within to determine the right path.

The heart considers the two jobs and which one might best serve our personal growth. It soothes the emotions with the reminder that it will choose what is best. As the mind starts strategizing to address the concerns of the emotions, the heart will consider which job provides not only financial security, but also a good working environment in which we can grow. The heart will calmly listen for God's voice and make the decision based on what it intuits is the right thing.

We benefit from these three guides by thinking, being aware, and testing the ideas they offer with the reality around us. Remember what I shared about making my decision to go to the prison for work? My emotions were aroused with excitement about a change. Then, when other people encouraged me not to consider it, my mind took into account their fears for me, and I tried to back off. My heart made it clear this was the right direction for me even though there was information suggesting it would be very hard and challenging. Making the right choice required my willingness to listen, think, and act on what these guiding forces indicated were God's intention for me.

～ის～

To surrender to God means keeping ourselves in a place of open communion with Him and responding to what we experience with trust in His intentions for us. There is a story told in many traditions where a man inherits a fine horse. All of his neighbors tell him what wonderful luck he has. He just says, "We'll see, we'll see." A little while later, his son is riding the horse and falls off, breaking his leg. The neighbors say what a terrible tragedy this is. Again, the man says, "We'll see, we'll see." A war breaks out in that country and the king sends out his soldiers to forcibly recruit all the eligible young men. When they come to the man's home they find his son with a broken leg and leave him behind.

If we let our minds and emotions control us, we will be on a constant roller coaster of turmoil and poor choices. The false self reacts to these two by choosing what will best preserve its self. It will feed on the anxieties of the emotions and work toward selfish ends. The heart accepts what is, staying even, clear, and open. It chooses its response from a deep place of spiritual connection and wisdom. It surrenders to the present moment and moves into the next moment with thoughtfulness and understanding.

20

Bread Labor

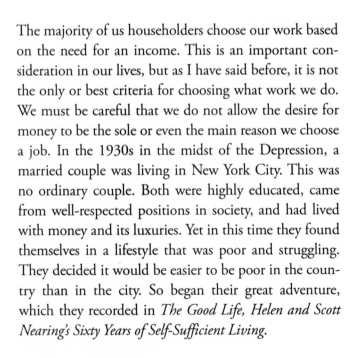

The majority of us householders choose our work based on the need for an income. This is an important consideration in our lives, but as I have said before, it is not the only or best criteria for choosing what work we do. We must be careful that we do not allow the desire for money to be the sole or even the main reason we choose a job. In the 1930s in the midst of the Depression, a married couple was living in New York City. This was no ordinary couple. Both were highly educated, came from well-respected positions in society, and had lived with money and its luxuries. Yet in this time they found themselves in a lifestyle that was poor and struggling. They decided it would be easier to be poor in the country than in the city. So began their great adventure, which they recorded in *The Good Life, Helen and Scott Nearing's Sixty Years of Self-Sufficient Living*.

The Nearings began a homesteading pioneer project of living simply, healthfully, and creatively. It was a life that fulfilled a yearning and dream in their hearts and inspired many others. They chose how to live and lived within their limits without resentment or feeling in any way deprived. They were more alive, healthy, and happy than most people of their time or today.

They make the point that because we live in a money economy, we have to have a cash crop. We have to have some financial income for the things we cannot make or create ourselves, and to be responsible to government institutions, e.g. taxes. They called the work they did to cover this need their bread labor.

The Nearings divided their time between the things they valued. Bread labor was given four hours of the day. The labor they chose contributed to the world's physical work. Their first endeavor was to make maple syrup from the trees on their land in Vermont. When they moved to Maine they grew blueberries. Another four hours of their day they gave to professional activities such as writing, lecturing, and teaching. The last four hours of the day they dedicated to civic activities. They met with others to participate in the survival and well-being of the world. They started and joined organizations. People often came to stay with them in order to live and learn their lifestyle. Within these guidelines for their days they canned their own food, played musical instruments, and hiked the natural beauty around them.

As we become more holy, we will want our use of time and money to reflect what we value. The Nearings chose a lifestyle that allowed them to contribute to what they valued. How many of us are doing the same? If we value our family, are we spending time with them? Do we use our money to help them grow and develop? Does our use of time and money contribute to the well-being of those we love, the world, and ourselves? Or are we using our time and money to avoid thinking too much about our lives, losing ourselves in entertainment, indulgence, or competing with our neighbors?

St. Paul worked as a tent maker and supported himself as he nurtured the church. His suggestion is:

> *Make it your intention to lead a quiet life, to mind your own business and to work with your hands, just as we told you, so that your daily life may win the respect of outsiders and so that you will not be dependent on anybody.* (1 Thessalonians 4:11-12, NIV)

We need bread labor in order to fulfill our responsibilities and to pursue those things necessary for a well-balanced life. At the same time, we must not allow our lives to be dominated by making money, believing it is the only way to be fulfilled, secure, respected, or to have power. We do well to choose work that reflects who we are and who we want to be in the world. Our work needs to satisfy our responsibility to give back, to be creative, and to be holy.

As we work toward fulfilling our dreams and passions, we may have to work in bread labor jobs that do not appear to fit our spiritual intentions, but they still serve a purpose in our process of growth and evolution. They are not the completion of what we have to contribute, but they may be perfect for this time in our lives. We must accept where we are at this moment, but as we grow, we will re-evaluate and consider what we truly need. We will discern and intuit how this differs from what the false self tells us we must have. When we do the work of discernment we can begin to make choices that better align with God's intentions for us. Then we will be living the adventure. Our lives are our work, a work that is full of surprises, joys, and satisfaction.

21

Money

Money is a symbol for what we get in return for the energy we put into our work. Jean-Luc Picard, the captain of the Enterprise in the *Star Trek* TV and movie series, tells a character in one of the movies that in the future where he lives, money is no longer the item of trade by which they negotiate getting and having. With the electronic age coming so fully into our financial dealings, we can already see that the paper and coin forms are becoming obsolete.

In places where money has been scarce people have bartered for things, worked for food and shelter, traded goods and labor. Such exchanges of energy create more intimate connections with our community and those with whom we live. We become more aware of the web of life. Using money separates us from the awareness of what it represents, which is our life energy. In consequence, we can lose track of what it costs us to get the money we have. When we realize that we spend hours of our life doing something in order to get a certain amount of money, we have to question if the life energy we have expended is worth what we got back for it.

God deals in life energy, not money. He cares very much what we do with our life energy. God is focused on uniting us with Him and with each other in love. He would have us use our life energy in the service of this purpose. What we get back is abundance. An abundant life does not depend on money.

Some of the most abundant times in my life were also the times I had the least money. When I left my first marriage, I had very little material wealth. However, I followed my dreams and felt great freedom and joy in going to graduate school. I worked as a waitress and found that this perfectly balanced the work I did for school. I always had everything I needed. However, God did test me.

The restaurant where I was working closed down. I decided to wait to look for another job for a month so I could study for master's level exams, which I had to pass before going on for my PhD. Once those were completed, I began my search. I had never had any problem finding work. I interviewed at two different jobs that were suitable, but they did not hire me. I was surprised, but continued to search. No other jobs seemed appropriate or right for me.

My money began to get very low and I had to ask my landlord to accept half the rent at the beginning of the month because I did not have it all. This really freaked me out. I truly believed that God provides everything I need, so I began to question what I was doing wrong that God was not answering my prayers for help.

I became so distraught by this I went to a spiritual counselor to ask what she might suggest, since I knew I must be missing something spiritually. What she did was extremely practical. She gave me money. This shocked me. It also made me very grateful.

As I came to the end of the month, within the same week, the first two places where I had interviewed both called and offered me jobs. This was not an accident. It provided a life lesson that has stayed with me. God was making it clear that He would provide what was needed when the time was right. All my anxiety and stress were pointless. God's timing is not my timing, but He provides what I need when I need it. Even the generosity of my spiritual counselor was part of God's plan and message. It reminded me that God works through others, and that generosity is an important key to how the world works.

Our attitude about money will have a great deal

of influence over how we handle it. If we are always afraid there will not be enough, then there will never be enough no matter how much we have. If we do not trust God to provide what we need, we will always feel we must work harder, control everything more tightly, and live in constant fear that we cannot get enough. When we live this way we cannot afford to be generous. Remember Lenedra Carroll's vision of the web of life. Too many of us live in this tight fear about money, so the amount of abundance or life energy that passes between us and the rest of the world becomes a trickle rather than the flowing stream it is meant to be.

22

Tithing

Marc Allen in his book *The Ten Percent Solution* tells an entertaining story that guides us to give ten percent of our income to ourselves through savings, give ten percent away in a tithe back into the world, and learn to live in partnership with others working together to solve the world's problems. This is good spiritual wealth management.

Tithing, giving back to God ten percent of all that comes to us, is one of the most powerful spiritual disciplines we householders can do. There were times in my first marriage that I tithed my income, but I still had my husband's income to live on. I did not even consider tithing when I was in graduate school. Then I read a book called *I'm Rich Beyond My Wildest Dreams, I am. I am. I am.* Thomas L. Pauley and his daughter, Penelope J. Pauley, write about how to live abundantly.

At that time I was in private practice and making

just enough money to live and pay my responsibilities. I feared tax season most of all because I was never sure if I had given enough money to the IRS. As I read the Pauley's chapter on tithing, I found myself crying great salty tears. A huge surge of energy ran through my body and I felt a kind of excited disbelief. I remember thinking, "Am I really going to do this?"

It suddenly seemed like the only right thing to do. God was giving me a clear message. It felt like a leap into a dark, frightening abyss. There was no cutting corners or finding a way around ten percent of my gross income. I felt God's resounding "yes" in my gut as I asked if He really wanted me to do this.

As I said at the beginning of this book, I have always struggled with how to be holy while living in the world. My fantasies were based on reading about holy people who had lived without material wealth, depending on God for all their worldly needs. What I realized was that tithing is the way we householders live that holy dependence on God. It is our reminder that everything we have is a gift from Him. The life energy for which I get money, and the money itself all belong to God. As Job states in the Old Testament:

Naked I came from my mother's womb, and naked I will depart. The Lord gave and the Lord has taken away; may the name of the Lord be praised.
(Job 1:20, NIV)

The truth is that God can provide whatever is needed without our money. Tithing is about us, and how we choose to live. Deuteronomy 14:23 states:

Bring this tithe to the place the Lord your God chooses for his name to be honored.... The purpose of tithing is to teach you always to fear the Lord your God. (NLT)

"Fear" is the awe, overwhelming love, and deep respect that come to us when we see God working directly in our lives. Never in these many years of tithing have I ever lacked for anything I needed or wanted. Always, somehow, my finances seem to work themselves out, often in surprising ways.

Over and over God has shown me He is in control of my wealth and abundance in life. God cares about me, and how I am growing and developing in Him. True abundance is found in a life well-lived, trusting in God, and living aligned with God's will.

We need to be conduits in this world. What comes to us needs also to flow out of us. We need to give as well as receive in order to live lives of abundance. As Marc Allen shows us in his formula of ten percent, our tithe is not just about money. It is also about giving of our time and giving to ourselves. When we live

TITHING

generously in every area of our lives, we are acknowledging our dependence on God and our trust in Him. Letting our life energy flow freely is rewarded with God's life energy flowing back to us.

23

Abundance

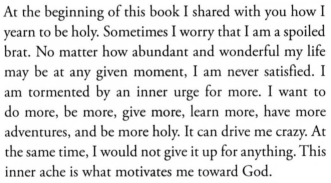

At the beginning of this book I shared with you how I yearn to be holy. Sometimes I worry that I am a spoiled brat. No matter how abundant and wonderful my life may be at any given moment, I am never satisfied. I am tormented by an inner urge for more. I want to do more, be more, give more, learn more, have more adventures, and be more holy. It can drive me crazy. At the same time, I would not give it up for anything. This inner ache is what motivates me toward God.

What I have come to understand is that this inner urge for more is a very natural response to aligning my will with God's will. God is the Creator. What God does is create. In consequence, as I become more like God, formed in His image, the more I am going to feel the need to create as well. The more attuned to God we are, the more we take on this need to expand, grow, become, and create. That is God's heart reflected in our own. Jesus tells us:

> *I am come that they might have life, and that*
> *they might have it more abundantly.* (John 10:10
> King James Version)

So many of our faith traditions seem to teach that we should reject the world, and make ourselves small, sacrificial, and poor. There is good reason for this. Our desires are often distorted by an unhealthy attachment to the things of this world dominated by our false self needs. If we focus on the negative, then rejecting the objects of our desire in order to manage our unhealthy attachments makes sense.

What if we were to focus on the positive instead? We would look to our potential, to the good in the world and ourselves, and to the desires of the true self. What is right and true naturally draws us to greater fulfillment of God's intentions for us. Rather than focusing on our failures, we could focus on success and allow ourselves to be drawn toward it. After all, holiness is about being successfully united with God.

‟∞‟

On a fine fall day I was hiking in the hills above my home, lost in the meditative thinking that comes from a steady pace in a quiet, beautiful place. I was pondering the issue of gratitude. Playing in my mind was the thought that it is not happy people who are grateful, but grateful people who are happy. The Pauleys, whose book I mentioned above, had said it is not wealthy people who tithe, but people who tithe that are wealthy. I put my own words to this concept. It felt deeply true.

Toying with this a bit, I realized it meant that gratitude breeds joy. Immediately on the heels of that thought flashed the idea that joy breeds generosity. Then it went a step further to the idea that generosity breeds creativity. I got a rush of gratefulness and happiness, since I love this kind of thinking where my thoughts carry me into new ideas that vibrate with truth.

When we focus our attention on gratitude for what we have, the ways in which we are growing and the blessings that come to us, our hearts are filled with a peaceful overflowing joy. The joy makes us feel so good and so full that we become inspired to share that joy with others, hence generosity. Such a joy cannot be kept within. It absolutely requires a way to flow outward. Clogged joy nearly explodes our insides, and sours if we cannot find a way to express it. Joy is a warm fuzzy and can maintain itself only by being given away.

Finding ways to express and share our joy spurs creativity. Because shared joy is much richer than a private joy we hug to ourselves, we become inspired to come up with creative ways to put it into a form we can share. Creativity is endless. Do not limit creativity by thinking it can be expressed only in one area or one kind of production. We can make and create art, food, and friendships. I enjoy creating ideas to share. As we become Holy Householders, we are creating a conduit for our true selves to be shared with the world. Are you feeling the gratitude and joy of this yet?

∽∂ᚪ

When we focus on the positive, abundance flows to us. This is the theme of many teachers. I have already mentioned W.D. Wattles, Shakti Gawain, Marc Allen, Lenedra Carroll, and Thomas and Penelope Pauley. They teach us a way to draw God's abundance to ourselves, and to fulfill God's purpose for us. The New Age literature calls this manifestation.

My take on it is that *the first step in the process is to get clear on what it is we want.* We must listen to our hearts, sit with this, and come to know what our desires are. Since God plants His desires for us in our hearts, the things we come up with from this honest place will come from what God desires for us. They will reflect our passions and our gifts. Attaining these things—whether they are material goods, work opportunities, experiences, or relationships—will reflect the abundance God desires for us.

The second step is to hold the idea of what we want

in our minds and hearts in detail. It is suggested that we focus on one thing at a time. Write it down, imagine already having it, and visualize it clearly. In this way we are inviting God to put into form that which He has planted as a desire in our hearts. These details will help us to recognize the clues and opportunities that God provides to lead us to receiving what it is we want.

The third step is to let it go. Leave it up to God how He chooses to honor this desire. We cannot control the process. As I said before, I do not want to be the master of my universe. God knows what is good and right for me and for everyone else. By giving our desire to God, we are acknowledging our dependence and trust in Him. The Pauleys in their book *I'm Rich Beyond My Wildest Dreams, I am. I am. I am.* tell us to write a specific sentence at the beginning of our journals that gives the whole process to the Divine for the good of all.

The fourth step is to keep alert and respond to the opportunities that arise that lead us to that for which we have asked. We need to follow through on ideas, intuitions, or inspirations that come. We have to act on what comes to us in order to receive what is being offered.

My husband and I had been thinking about getting a dog since our previous dog had died a few years before. Several times when we were near the animal shelter we thought of going in, but did not feel overly motivated and got distracted. Costco, the warehouse store, is very near the shelter, so when we went there I would think about it. On one particular day I had thought of it, but dismissed it, thinking my husband would not want to take the time. As we were leaving Costco he suddenly asked if I wanted to go to the animal shelter. It seemed significant to me that we had both thought of it so I said, "Why not?" As soon as we walked into the kennels there she was. We both knew almost immediately this was the dog for us. Our desire for a dog had been growing and the thought was clearly there in our minds and hearts. God knew just the right dog for us for the good of all.

⤫

God has work for us to do. He has a purpose for us. There is no reason we should ever doubt that He will provide everything we need in order to fulfill this work.

> *And God is able to make all grace abound to you, so that in all things at all times, having all that you need, you will abound in every good work.*
> (2 Corinthians 9:8, NIV)

One day as I was coming to the end of my hike in the hills above my house God gave me the inner impression that He wanted me to pick up trash when I hiked. I did not like this idea. The trash is dirty, it would distract from my meditative focus, and I did not want to have to carry something in my hands.

I tried to dismiss the thought, but God pressed against me and I knew He really meant it. Feeling guilty about my resistance, I gave myself in full surrender to this idea and began carrying a plastic grocery bag with me on my walks.

One day I decided to walk a bigger loop from my house higher into the hills. By the time I got to the top, my plastic bag was overflowing. One more thing I put in ripped a slice in the side of it. I had to carry the top and the split pinched together to hold the trash in. The road before me was closer to the housing area and had more traffic than the others, so I knew there would be more trash there.

Turning to God, I told Him that if He wanted me to continue to pick up trash, He was going to have to provide me with another bag. I specified that it would need to be a bag bigger than a grocery bag because I would need to put the bag I now held into it as well as any new trash.

A few more steps ahead I noticed something white lying under the bushes by the side of the road. As I got closer, I paused in amazement. Under the bush was a kitchen-sized trash bag. It was neatly folded as though it had been taken straight out of its box and laid there on purpose. It had minimal dew and small specks of dirt on the outside of it, but it had never been unfurled. It was brand new and unused.

ABUNDANCE

A shot of electric energy coursed through my body. Awe, gratitude, and joy flooded my senses and brought tears to my eyes. I felt overwhelmed by God's generosity, kindness, and personal interest in even the smallest details of the work He had given me to do. If God is willing to provide for something so small and insignificant, what more will He provide for the big projects He asks of us in life?

I want to share one more bag story because it is such a good example of God's sense of humor. On another walk I forgot to take a bag with me. I apologized to God when I realized, but in my heart I felt relief and some naughtiness as I thought I had innocently outsmarted God on this one walk. Then I looked ahead, and there on a dead weed was a plastic grocery bag. Its handles were wrapped around the weed like a flag on a flagpole and it was waving merrily in the breeze.

❦

We are raised with the idea that there is not enough. Remember the story of the warm fuzzies versus the cold pricklies. It is deeply ingrained in us that we must work hard for everything we have, and we must compete with everyone else for what there is. As long as we think this way, it will be true. As long as we believe that the only way to get abundance is to take it from the other guy, we will feel some inner uncertainty and maybe even shame about wanting anything for ourselves. It will feel selfish. At the same time, we have the God-given desire for abundance for ourselves. The battle inside over this may make us shut down our inner voice and just go for what we want, thinking this is the only way to get it. Or we may give up on wanting anything and live a limited life.

What we have to understand is that there is no limit to what God can provide from His end. It is our spiritual immaturity that keeps us from receiving the benefits of God's abundance. W.D. Wattles in his book *The Science of Getting Rich* makes a distinction between creative versus competitive gain. When we live from a creative place, everyone benefits. There are no limits. When we are stuck in competitive tactics, we take from the other more than we give. We take at their expense. In creative gain, what we take is balanced by what we give. We promote the flow within the web of life. For example, if I own a business but I can pay my employees only minimum wage, I can offer creative compensations such as flexible time, opportunities to promote, and a friendly, safe atmosphere. In this way everyone can live more abundantly.

❧

How many really rich people have you known or heard about who are happy? When I read the entertainment magazines I am amazed at the mess people's lives have become. They have excessive wealth, popularity, attention, and material goods—yet their lives are painfully unbalanced. They appear to be living a competitive life of not enough, so they are never satisfied. They are ruled by the needs of the false self and interpret abundance from that perspective. To me, their spirits look starved.

There are people who appear stuck in a poor life. They cannot imagine anything else. They do not believe they can have the abundance that is around them. Altruistic people who give their time and money to setting up sustainable lifestyles for the poor have always impressed me. These people help build wells, plant gardens, offer education, provide small loans, and show the poor how to improve their lives in a way that they can develop on their own. The altruistic workers provide hope and address what the poor can have rather than what they do not have. They focus on positive potential and offer ways to make that possible.

Abundance is about living life to the fullest. It is about having everything we need and want to be God's people in the world. This may or may not require material wealth. Many saints chose to live in simple poverty, but still had everything they needed to live the abundance to which God called them. Their life purpose was fulfilled by this simplicity. Abraham lived the householder life with great wealth and still lived the life to which God called him. We householders have a choice. For most of us, our choices so far have reflected our hearts' desires to be in the world, living among people, having intimate relationships, children, pets, homes, and bounty to share with others. Doing this as God's people, God's way makes us Holy Householders.

When we live in the way I have been talking about throughout this book, God can provide everything we need to live an abundant, blessed, and good life. Out of this kind of life, we can give back to the world freely. Abundance happens as we let our wealth flow in and let our wealth flow out. We are limited only by what we imagine is necessary for us to live the life we are meant to have. As we filter out our false self needs, our idea of abundance will adjust to the callings of our true self. As we learn to ask, we will receive. God will show us the way.

> *Seek ye first the kingdom of God, and his righteousness; and all these things shall be added unto you.* (Matthew 6:33, King James Version)

Section V
Health

24

Body, Mind, and Spirit

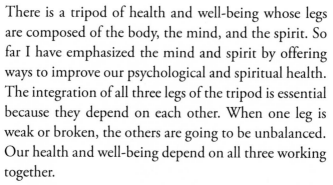

There is a tripod of health and well-being whose legs are composed of the body, the mind, and the spirit. So far I have emphasized the mind and spirit by offering ways to improve our psychological and spiritual health. The integration of all three legs of the tripod is essential because they depend on each other. When one leg is weak or broken, the others are going to be unbalanced. Our health and well-being depend on all three working together.

Suppose we put all our energy into our bodies—exercising, eating healthy, and adorning ourselves attractively—but do nothing for our mind or spirit. When the mind and spirit legs of the tripod are under-nourished, we tend to live on the surface of life. We have no idea what goes on within our own hearts. We do not listen to our intuition or struggle for discernment. Our thinking will tend toward concrete interpretations of the world. We will have no interest in or awareness of the deeper meaning of things. Our relationships will be shallow, our behaviors controlled and robotic, and though our work may be meticulous, it will lack imagination and creativity.

What if we work hard at developing our minds but ignore our spiritual and physical health? We may be intellectually gifted, comprehend how things work, especially their technical meanings, and may provide valuable contributions to the world through new ideas or helpful mechanical improvements. However, our ideas may result in negative contributions without our realizing or caring what we have done. The master we serve and the voice to which we listen will not be God's.

Remember when I spoke of how the mind wants to take care of business and cares little for relationships or what is right and true? When the mind is our main area of strength we may create new military weapons for destruction, develop genetically altered foods that help make money for the industry but lack the nutrient values needed, or argue for new laws that address a specific problem but lack compassion and awareness of larger consequences.

When we are dominated by our intellect, intimacy can be incomprehensible and frightening. Our emotions are usually shut down so tight that we cannot put words to how we feel and come to believe feelings are pointless. Our bodies will seem irrelevant until they start to break down. Arrogance is a great risk for us because our emphasis on our mind is the place the false self has flourished, while our true self is silenced. We can become completely numb to our need for the other two legs of the tripod.

Many clients come to therapy because of the breakdown in their relationships. The reason for this is often their tendency to live in their heads to the exclusion of their feelings. They do not share or even allow themselves to be aware of their feelings. Their hearts are foreign territory, which they would rather not explore. They usually come to therapy because their significant other is threatening to leave. It is a very scary place for them. Building trust with such clients requires going slowly. They need their defenses and must be helped to learn to open to the other legs of the tripod so they can let go of their defenses a little at a time.

Lastly, if we focus exclusively on our spiritual lives we may gain spiritual power and followers, but our bodies and our minds will be weak. We have all heard of spiritually advanced leaders who got caught in inappropriate sexual liaisons or who spent excessive money on indulgences. Two come to mind right now: Jimmy Swaggart, the Christian televangelist who was caught having liaisons with prostitutes after having publicly condemned two other televangelists for sexually inappropriate behavior; and Bhagwan Shree

Rajnesh currently known as Osho, the Indian mystic guru who was alleged to have had over fifty Rolls-Royce automobiles and was called the "sex guru" in the media. Although they appear to be in touch with a higher power and may preach a good sermon, their behavior suggests they are out of touch with God and with people. They appear to be focused on the spirit through their false self and to be underdeveloped in the other areas of health and well-being. Their weaknesses usually catch up with them, leaving a trail of spiritual disillusionment in their wake.

> *Woe to you Pharisees, because you give God a tenth of your mint, rue and all other kinds of garden herbs, but you neglect justice and the love of God. You should have practiced the latter without leaving the former undone.* (Luke 11:42, NIV)

❧❧

Spiritual teachers often suggest that the disciplines for the body are the easiest to undertake, but I find them to be one of the hardest. For us householders, eating and physical activities are social events. We eat with our families, friends, coworkers, business associates, church and community members, and organizational affiliates. Consider Rotary club dinners and potlucks. This means the management of what we eat becomes a more challenging and awkward endeavor. When teachers like W.D. Wattles tell us to eat only when we are hungry and only the food natural to our region we may agree, but doubt our ability to accomplish such a task.

The great demands for our time and energy as householders often makes a regular exercise program feel like an overwhelming chore. It is easier to watch TV with our family than to get our spouse and children to go outside and ride bikes together. We may feel guilty taking time away from them if we want to start some physical activity on our own. As I have discussed before, it can be hard to choose what is right for us without feeling we are somehow disappointing the other people in our lives.

At the same time, it is critical that we be aware of the health of our physical bodies. When we are over or underfed, our minds become sluggish and distracted. The messages of the Spirit are difficult to hear when we are physically in distress. When our bodies are in pain or out of balance we have trouble concentrating on anything else. Our whole world can be taken over by the demands of medical interventions and the inability to do the things we want to do.

Our bodies are the way we interact in this material world. Like the suits astronauts wear in space or on the moon, we need this physical form in order to participate in the world in which we live and have our being. The healthier our bodies, the freer we are to put our energy into nurturing the other legs of the tripod. When all three legs of the tripod are in balance we are able to live in a way that brings joy, gratitude, and abundance to our lives.

25

Appetites

Appetite is the desire to satisfy a craving or need. In and of itself appetite is a good thing. We need certain things to live and regenerate. Desiring those things in order to survive and flourish is a perfectly natural part of being human and alive. When our tripod of health and well-being is in balance, well-nourished, and our healthy appetites are satisfied, we live more fulfilling lives. We live exactly as God intended. The Garden of Eden in the Old Testament is an example of this. God made an incredibly abundant environment with plants, animals, and rivers for man. He made man in His own image so that man could be one with Him. He partnered man with woman so he would not be alone. He put man in the garden to "work it and take care of it" (Genesis 2:15, NIV). Every need of body, mind, and spirit were met, including our need for work and relationships.

When our tripod of health and well-being is not in balance, our appetites go bad. What we believe we need and what we crave can become distorted and destructive. Often the appetites are an attempt to rebalance ourselves, but the distortion confuses the whole effort. We saw this when I talked about the false self behaviors that are used to help us feel secure, loved, and in control. The more insecure, unloved, and out of control we feel, the more intensely we experience our appetites. When we use the behaviors of the false self to feel better, we end up with more cravings and hunger.

⁖

Patty had always been a little overweight. Her mother would try to limit her diet by not buying sweets and feeding her salads, but whenever Patty left the house she stocked up on candy, cookies, and chips. Her father would take her older sister out to shop for clothes, but told Patty until she lost weight he was not willing to invest in her.

When Patty went to college she was introduced to methamphetamines, an illegal drug that gave her energy and took away her appetite. She began to use this drug a lot. Her parents came to visit her and were very complimentary about how good she looked because she was quite slender. They did not seem to notice the slight yellowing of her eyes and teeth. All they noticed was her weight.

Patty craved their approval and soon began to crave the drug. Without it she would become lethargic, irritable, and depressed. After a while, even with the drug she found her depression growing and the high less pleasant. However, she stayed skinny, so she thought it was the right thing for her.

Patty was out of balance in her life and she knew it. She knew her eating habits were not healthy. She knew she did not like herself. The cravings and desires of her heart were to be loved, accepted, and to feel good about herself. Her true self, the Spirit within her, was crying out for her to fulfill these essential needs. The drug she used to try to answer that cry was unhealthy and destructive. Drugs could not solve her problems nor give her what she needed, but they gave her some relief without requiring that she work very hard to get it.

❧

Giving in to unhealthy appetites always comes back to hurt us. No matter how much we try to satisfy our needs with false appetites, we always end up starving and craving more. As we can see in Patty's example, the false self is a big part of our not following through on what is right for our physical well-being. Our motivations and our energy get sidetracked from what is healthy for us into what the false self is telling us will meet our needs. In her case, the only thing the false self cared about was looking slender so she could get her parents' approval. When we open to the Spirit and take our first courageous steps toward living our lives from our true self, our motivation toward health increases.

The more we are able to align our appetites to what we know is healthy, the more balanced will be our tripod of health and well-being. Most of the holy people about whom I have read have addressed the need to manage our appetites. As we work to live healthy, abundant lives we too will need to manage ourselves and what we put into our bodies and what we do with them. It is easy to indulge our senses with food, drugs, sex, and adrenaline. As we grow more holy as householders, we will apply our creativity and our wills toward finding ways to integrate healthy appetites into our daily lives. By doing so we also encourage and support the people we love toward these healthy behaviors.

> *...when we find peace within there will be no more conflict, no more occasion for war. If this is the peace you seek,* **purify your body** *by sensible living habits,* **purify your mind** *by expelling all negative thoughts,* **purify your motives** *by casting out any ideas of greed or self-striving and by seeking to serve your fellow human beings,* **purify your desires** *by eliminating all wishes for material possessions or self-glorification and*

*by desiring to know and do God's will for you.
Inspire others to do likewise.* (*Peace Pilgrim Her
Life and Work in Her Own Words*, bold letter-
ing is mine)

26

Fasting

Fasting and prayer are jewels in our spiritual treasury. Fasting is the letting go of that to which we are attached in order to make more room for God and our health. Often fasting and prayer are done together because fasting helps purify our attention, bodies, and energy, which when purified allow us to open more freely to the Spirit within us. By emptying ourselves of attachments we create space for God to fill. When our tripod of health is off balance and our appetites are out of control, fasting can realign both, like a chiropractor adjusting our spines.

By refusing to give in to indulgences, cravings, and our often mistaken beliefs about what we need we take back our God-given power, we develop patience, humility, willpower, and self-esteem, as well as clarity, attention, and health. Fasting usually awakens us to a deeper spiritual connectedness with God, others, and ourselves. Partly this is due to our focusing our attention. When we fast, we are very aware of what we are not allowing ourselves to have and the reason we are not allowing ourselves to have it. By letting go of things to which we are attached, we also free ourselves from their power over us. It is suggested that fasting can even break addictions.

I have a particularly unhealthy relationship with sugar. Usually I keep it under control. However, during Halloween, Christmas, and Easter I often become overwhelmed by temptation. For a while I had office space in a medical doctor's office. Pharmaceutical representatives would come to sell their wares and leave piles of sweets behind to tempt the office staff into supporting their cause. One Halloween all my favorite candy bars were represented, along with fresh fudge, brownies, and cookies. Every time I went past them I compulsively ate some more. I remember thinking "I have got to stop this." I felt queasy, light-headed, and grumpy, but still I would eat another Snickers.

The power our addictions have over us can be very scary. When I fast from food it always includes sugar. I fast during certain designated religious periods, but I also do sugar fasts after each of the holidays just to get myself back. Oddly enough, after a few days of fasting from sugar I no longer crave it. My body cleans up and I start enjoying healthy food more. I have more energy and think more clearly. I stop getting sick as often. You would think I would stop eating sugar as a way of life, but it has a way of creeping up on me, as all addictions tend to do.

Refusing food is not the only way to fast. There are many attachments we have in life that keep us distracted and unaware. In honor of a religious period of fasting I did not allow myself to buy a book for six weeks. I am very attached to books. Even though I have many of them I am always buying more. A few hours browsing in Barnes and Noble bookstore is a delight, but it can get expensive. Due to my book fast I read fewer "toy" books and focused instead on spiritually and intellectually stimulating reading.

❧

Fasting is promoted in every major religion. Christianity especially encourages fasting during Lent, the six weeks before Easter, as an alignment with Christ who fasted for forty days before he started his ministry. Ramadan is the Islamic month of fasting where Muslims refrain from eating and drinking during the day. It aligns with the month in which the first verses of the Qur'an were revealed to the prophet Muhammad. Judaism, Hinduism, and Buddhism also encourage fasting.

Fasting builds our character. When we struggle (fasting is a struggle), we challenge ourselves for a higher good. We are choosing to sacrifice what we think we want in order to achieve something we know we need. This letting go of one thing to make room for another often brings amazing gifts into our lives. We often experience what are called breakthroughs.

We householders can especially feel stuck, unsure of what choices to make, what directions to go. We have so many choices and opportunities available to us, at the same time we may feel trapped by the demands and responsibilities in our lives. We can feel confused and frustrated, yearning to break through the stuck feeling and to hear God's voice in our hearts so that we can act. Fasting is a way to promote our ability to hear God's voice amidst the turmoil in our lives. As we let go of the ways in which we numb and satisfy our senses, our spirits become more alert. We become more intuitively aware and can better focus our imagination on the way we want our life to be.

When my husband and I were still living in Los Angeles, we decided to take on a discipline of prayer in which we meditated for an hour every morning and an hour every night. This required a fast from sleep—we had to get up an hour earlier in the morning in order to get to work on time—and a fast at night from watching movies or reading as much as we had been.

We did this because we knew we wanted a change in our lives but were not sure what direction to go or what to do. We wanted to leave the city and live in the mountains. After three months of this additional prayer, our lives took a completely new turn. We had visited my husband's family in the northwest and flown back into Burbank airport horrified by the contrast between the rich, lush green of Washington State and the dry, brown, polluted atmosphere we flew into. Through a number of odd coincidences, such as not being scheduled at work the day we thought we were, and getting the newspaper when an ad came up for mountain property, we were able to visit the mountain town in which we now live.

Those three months of increased prayer and fasting drew to us the very changes we were wanting. Would they have happened if we had not prayed and fasted? I do not think so. We would not have been as fortified or clear. We might not have had the courage or certainty to pursue the opportunities that arose. Because of our fasting and praying, we were prepared to follow the steps of manifestation before we knew anything about them.

Fasting helps us take leaps in our spiritual life. It also strengthens us for the steady pace of growth and evolution that is our spiritual birthright. It helps us discern our weaknesses and strengths, and cleans up our bodies, minds, and spirits so that we can go forward with enthusiasm and energy.

We must choose our fasts thoughtfully and be sure our purposes in doing them are clear and healthy. We will fail in our fasts if we are trying to prove something or impress someone else. We will be wasting our time and energy if we do not focus the fast on increased alignment with the Divine and our spiritual-physical health. Fasting is a gift given by grace to help us in our spiritual journey. Rather than thinking of it as a negative, a refusal of our desires, acknowledge it as a doorway to greater abundance and health.

27

Positive Thinking

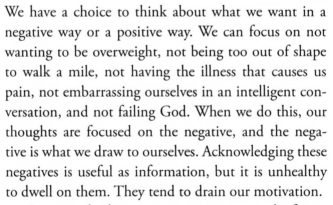

We have a choice to think about what we want in a negative way or a positive way. We can focus on not wanting to be overweight, not being too out of shape to walk a mile, not having the illness that causes us pain, not embarrassing ourselves in an intelligent conversation, and not failing God. When we do this, our thoughts are focused on the negative, and the negative is what we draw to ourselves. Acknowledging these negatives is useful as information, but it is unhealthy to dwell on them. They tend to drain our motivation.

I suggest thinking in a more positive way by focusing on what we do want. When we put our thought energy into what we want rather than what we do not want, we are much more likely to receive what we desire in our lives. We can follow the pattern of manifestation that I mentioned in the chapter on abundance by figuring out what we want, imagining the details, giving it all to God, then following through on the ways in which we can participate in making it happen.

When my husband and I have projects we want to accomplish around our home, we have found that if we sit down with a cup of tea and hang out in the area where the project needs to get done, we become much more motivated. We start thinking about what we want it to look like, which leads to what materials we will need to make it happen. The next thing you know, we are making lists and plans. With lists and plans to follow, we get excited about going to Home Depot or the local nursery to get what we need. Without any foot-dragging at all we are actively engaged in the project and getting it done.

✌◌❧

Focusing positively on what we want, rather than negatively on what we do not want, is a much more pleasant way to approach what we need to change in our lives. If we want to lose weight, we can start imagining ourselves at the weight we want to be. If we have a picture of ourselves or someone else at that weight we can put it on the refrigerator. This is a great motivator to eat a healthy snack rather than grabbing the ice cream. It also helps to have only healthy snacks *that we enjoy* in our refrigerator.

I read a lot of health journals and magazines that tell me all about the foods that are good for my body. They provide appetizing pictures and recipes. When I focus on the appealing colors and options that healthy foods provide, and I start looking for items that are interesting as well as healthy in the grocery store, I no longer dwell on what I am not allowing myself to eat.

Rather than focusing on how we need to get into shape and what exercise to do in order to get there, we can focus on what activities we enjoy doing. Exercise is about moving our bodies and burning calories. There are a lot of ways to do this, many of which become so engaging that we forget we are exercising. I like *Sunset* magazine because it recommends all kinds of fun activities to do in the western part of the US where I live. For me, gardening, walking in the mountains or on the beach, riding my bike, and playing tennis or racquetball are play rather than work. Going to a gym or using stationary exercise equipment are boring and depressing for me. I would rather focus on positive, fun activities that give me the same benefits. Other people love going to the gym, where they can socialize and follow their progress more easily.

꩜

We are meant to enjoy our food and physical activities. We are meant to enjoy our lives. Choosing healthy options we enjoy is just as easy as choosing unhealthy ones, except for the habits we have formed. We get used to our pattern of living. We get up in the morning and have a cigarette with our coffee. We grab a donut and a latte on the way to work. We buy a burger for lunch or go out with friends for a pizza. We come home and have a drink while we catch up on the news. We may make dinner but use prepared foods that we just have to microwave or pop in the oven.

There are people who claim they have no time to cook or eat meals at home. Work, school, and after-school activities all demand every moment of their day. They also believe they cannot afford fresh grocery store food. Fast food is cheap and easy. We tend to be creatures of habit. It is easier to follow established patterns than to have to create new ones. It makes life more efficient and less stressful. Most of our habit patterns are unconsciously chosen. We do not plan them. Instead we just fall into them, and then keep them up out of habit. They are easy for us.

When these habits are destructive, we must rework them. Fasting, as discussed in the chapter above, can help us break out of the pattern so we can establish a new one. Once we have reworked and established healthy patterns, those healthy patterns will become easy, lower our stress, and make our time efficient. The hard part is changing our pattern. Getting up in the morning and going for a walk rather than a cigarette and coffee can at first feel very hard. After a while we begin to look forward to the fresh air, interesting sights, and good feeling in our bodies. At first, making lunches for our children to take to school and for ourselves to take with us to work may feel like a burden, but after we have done it for a while we begin to appreciate having good things to eat through out the day. We feel good about our children eating better. Healthy living provides its own rewards. Once the new habit is set, we just do it like we did the unhealthy one, but with much better results.

$$\backsim\!\infty\!\sim$$

 Approaching our lives positively and making changes from the motivation and energy that positive thinking provides seem to me the ways God intended us to live. It may be that some people need to embrace the negative in order to commit to change, but once the commitment is made, the positive focus is more helpful and productive.

 When our heart's desire is to have health in every aspect of our lives, our thoughts and behaviors will align themselves to this desire. However, we are very complex creatures. Our roads to health do not start out smooth, flat, or easy. Instead, they have boulders, potholes, twists, turns, steep grades, and slippery slopes.

 We do not start from a place of wholeness, but from a wounded place that has formed over years of living separately from God's intentions for the world and us. The good news is that our wounds can heal with God's help. Through our openness to divine love and intervention, our lives can move not just to wholeness, but also beyond it to abundance, prosperity, and holiness.

28

Conclusion

My intention in writing this book has been to encourage all of us to accept ourselves as we are right now and to move more deeply into relationship with God from that present place. Not everyone is called to be a traveling ascetic. To force ourselves into some role we think is holy is a danger to our spiritual lives. It leaves us vulnerable to the false self and the lies it tells us. Our role in this life is to be at the cutting edge of our own growth, fully participating in this moment in the life we are living. That means doing what we know to be right, and not doing what we know to be wrong. It also means opening and surrendering ourselves to God in love.

CONCLUSION

Writing this book has been a challenging and exciting adventure. When I was on a week-long silent meditation retreat I prayed, asking if I might have an angel help me write the book so it would reflect what God wanted me to write. I was reading Sophy Burnham's book on angel visitations at the time. I already had a first draft but I knew it was very incomplete. To my surprise, I got a strong affirmative sensation and immediately ideas started pouring in. I took some notes and thanked God for this special assurance.

I imagined seeing my book in a bookstore. I imagined myself presenting the material in workshops, bookstores, conferences, and retreats. Most of all I listened for God's guidance in writing it, and kept my heart open with gratitude. Whenever I hit a stuck place I would step back, give it a little time and meditation, and the answer would come to me rather than my having to chase after the answer. If you are reading this, it means you are sharing in the fruits of my manifested dream. I thought about it, imagined it, listened to God in my heart, and then did the work necessary to make it happen.

✌✌

Our hunger for God is our greatest gift. It keeps us alert and motivated to live the lives to which we are called. I do not believe our hunger is ever fully satisfied.

We never become complete, because we are all in creative process. There is always something more for us to do. Even the holiest of holy people are in process, because creating our lives is never-ending.

Life is an incredible adventure. Even the most difficult times are a valuable gift on the journey toward spiritual maturity. Through prayer, relationships, work, and health we live the rich blessings of our householder lives. I hope that reading this book has inspired and energized you to be a Holy Householder living your life prayerfully, joyfully, creatively, and gratefully. There is no better gift that I can give or receive. I take my place beside the saints, living my holiness from where I am right now, with my heart and mind open to God. So can you.

References, Permissions, and Copyrights

Allen, Marc. *The Ten Percent Solution, Simple Steps to Improve Our Lives & Our World*. Novata, California: New World Library, 2002. Copyright© 2002 by Marc Allen.

Bourgeault, Cynthia. *Encountering the Wisdom Jesus, Quickening the Kingdom of Heaven Within*. Boulder, CO: Sounds True. Copyright© 2005 Cynthia Bourgeault, (p) Sounds True.

Carroll, Lenedra J. *The Architecture of All Abundance, Creating a Successful Life in the Material World*. Novata, California: New World Library, 2001. Copyright© 2001 Lenedra Carroll.

Friends of Peace Pilgrim. *Peace Pilgrim Her Life and Work in Her Own Words*. Hemet, California: Ocean Tree Books, 1982, 1988. Copyright© 1982, 1988 Friends of Peace Pilgrim. Reprinted by permission of Friends of Peace Pilgrim.

Gawain, Shakti with Laurel King. *Living in the Light, A Guide to Personal and Planetary Transformation*. Novata, CA: Nataraj Publishing, a division of New

Kadloubovsky, E. and Palmer, G.E.H, translators. *Writings from the Philokalia on Prayer of the Heart.* London, Great Britain: Mackays of Chatham PLC, 1992. 1st published 1951 by Faber and Faber Limited.

Kazantzakis, Nikos. *St. Francis.* New York: A Touchstone Book published by Simon and Schuster, 1962. Copyright© 1962 by Simon & Schuster, Inc.

Keating, Thomas. *Invitation to Love, the Way of Christian Contemplation.* NY: The Continuum Publishing Co., 2001. Copyright© 1992 St. Benedict's Monastery.

Keating, Thomas. *Open Mind Open Heart. The Contemplative Dimension of the Gospel.* New York: Amity House, 1986. Copyright© 1986 by St. Benedict's Monastery.

Nearing, Helen and Scott. *The Good Life, Helen and Scott Nearing's Sixty Years of Self-Sufficient Living.* New York: Schocken Books Inc., 1970. Copyright© 1954 by Helen Nearing.

Pauley, Thomas L. & Pauley, Penelope J. *I'm Rich Beyond My Wildest Dreams, I am. I am. I am.* New York: Berkley Books, 1999. Copyright© 1999 by Thomas L. Pauley and Penelope J. Pauley.

Peck, MD, M. Scott. *The Road Less Traveled, A New Psychology of Love, Traditional Values, and Spiritual Growth.* New York: A Touchstone Book published by Simon & Schuster, 1978. Copyright© 1978 by M. Scott Peck, MD.

Steindl-Rast, David. *A Listening Heart, the Art of Contemplative Living.* New York: Crossroad, 1994. Copyright© 1983 by David Steindl-Rast.

Tolle, Eckhart. *A New Earth, Awakening to Your Life's Purpose*. Penguin audio, a member of Penguin Group (USA) Inc., and Books on Tape. Copyright© 2005 Eckhart Tolle, (p) 2005 Penguin Audio.

Wattles, Wallace D. *The Science of Being Great, Your Master Key to Success*. Blacksburg, VA: Wilder Publications, 2011. Copyright© 2011 Thrifty Books.

Yogananda, Paramahansa. *Man's Eternal Quest*. California: Self-Realization Fellowship, 1985. Copyright© 1982 Self-Realization Fellowship, reprinted 1985.